52 WORDS

THAT CAN CHANGE THE WAY
YOU LIVE IN THE WORLD

JASON TYNE

JEFF -

You ARE A LIVING
BREATHING MIRACLE !!
RIDE THE WAVE OF LIFE
+
PLAY BIG !!

DEDICATION

This book is dedicated to God, my family, my friends, and fellow learners in life. You are all living breathing miracles!

A deep gratitude of love to my wife Carrie, my son Davis and my daughter Brooke.

CONTENTS

ACKNOWLEDGMENTS

To my friends whom I value as a source of endless support:
Kelly Ritchie, Rick Lambrick, Jeff Levitan, Richard & Veronica Tan

A special acknowledgement to my great friend who spent endless
hours with me walking through the meadows of life, Bacchus.

52 WORDS

Getting the Most from This Book

I honestly believe that you are a living breathing miracle, predestined for greatness. Words have power. Words can build up or words can tear down. Your capacity will begin to increase as a result of you taking the time to pause and reflect on each of the 52 Words. This book is designed to walk you through one word per week over 52 weeks. Some of you may choose to move faster.

There are 6 sections for each word to guide you:

- **Definition:** Most people never take the time to truly understand the definition of words that they use everyday.

- **Bible Verse:** The bible is a source of eternal wisdom, whether you believe in the bible or not, you can find true power within it.

- **Food for Thought:** These are great ideas shared by wise people throughout time that have shaped and influenced my thinking.

- **Contemplation:** This is my commentary about the word based on my life experience. It is designed to get you to contemplate the word as it has played out in my life and others.

- **Empower Thought:** This section is designed to challenge and inspire you to move into action.

- **Questions to Ponder:** This section provides 3 questions for you to think deeply about and journal out your answers in detail. This is how you make your learning personal.

Ride the Wave of Life & PlayBig!!

Jason Tyne

Word 1: AFFECTION

Definition

A feeling of liking and caring for someone or something

Bible Verse

The Lord did not set His affection on you and choose you because you're more numerous than other peoples for you were the fewest of all peoples.
~ Deuteronomy 7:7 NIV

Food for Thought

We fear rejection, want attention, crave affection, and dream of perfection.
~ Anonymous

Contemplation

If we examine the above quote, "We fear rejection, want attention, crave affection, and dream of perfection". The three words of emphasis are rejection, attention and affection.

Now, let's take a step back and go to the dictionary definition of the word affection so that we can gain more clarity. The dictionary definition goes into the feeling of liking, caring or loving. This produces an outward projection of "you" to "somebody else", but the way I'd like you to consider this word isn't necessarily "you" to "somebody else". I'd like you to consider this word affection in terms of the opposite direction, that is, "somebody else" to "you". In other words, being able to *experience affection* your-self because once you can understand it from that perspective, you can begin to understand how it will feel for somebody else to receive affection.

Moving into the quote, "We fear rejection..." I believe all of us can relate to and understand that fear, the fear of rejection. Nobody ever wants to be rejected. Instead, we want attention, acceptance and affection.

We crave affection and dream of perfection. As we go through life, we begin to realize that we're not perfect and that we are broken. We begin to realize that there are things about us that we don't like and we realize that we have shortcomings. Hopefully those feelings lead us in a way that we want to grow. However, a lot of people get mislead with this dream of perfection. I believe that inside of everybody, there is a desire for an example of perfection out there, that there is something worth aspiring towards. We don't want to be sick. We don't want to be angry. We don't want to have negative thoughts and emotions. We don't want to get hurt. We don't want to cry. We don't want to experience the negative things. We'd just like to escape to this ultimate paradise of affection somehow.

What does it mean to "crave affection"? When you are hungry you crave food and you can't stop it. The craving just takes over and you become consumed by it and ultimately driven by it. Since we crave affection, something else takes over and we begin to have this constant internal hunger for something to satisfy us. Our spirit inside just wants to know that everything is going to be okay. In other words, we want to know that we're going to be loved regardless of what's going on.

Life has a way of throwing so many experiences and so many obstacles at us. These could include your health, your finances, your relationships, your knowledge, and your spiritual health. Everybody wakes up every single day, with a pile of problems staring him or her directly in the face. The challenge with problems is, that the moment you solve one problem, your reward for solving that problem is usually another bigger problem. Therefore, most people get discouraged and say, "...the more I solve my problems, the bigger my problems seem to get", becoming a huge demotivating factor. The truth is, you need to realize that you're probably on the right path, and the thing that is going to help you move through problems a little bit better is by understanding this word, affection.

Most people have a very difficult time in making a decision anywhere, in any area of their life. The reason most people have a hard time making a decision is because they have so much uncertainty. They are afraid that the decision that they are about to make is the wrong decision. They are afraid of making a mistake because that mistake might cause harm to them or somebody else. They become paralyzed from making a decision. That is why this word affection becomes extremely important to understand.

The more affection you have, the easier it will become to make a decision. The reason is if you have affection that's coming from someone or something bigger than you, it makes the ability to make decision easier. The certainty this provides you is that even if you happen to go down the wrong path, you're still going to be loved.

So when you have affection, making a decision becomes a little bit easier because the uncertainty starts to go away. Affection allows you to have the certainty in something much stronger.

∞

Empower Thought

If you crave affection, then most likely every other human that you come into contact with is most likely craving affection also. They too want certainty in their life. They too are seeking this dream of perfection. The challenge is to become a little bit more mindful of our own cravings for affection. As we do that, we begin to recognize that almost every other human is craving affection too. This creates a shift in the way that you live in the world. I hope that it does and I hope that you take the time and just sit on this word and contemplate its impact.

Questions to Ponder

1. When you think of what is going on in the world, what does this word make you think about? Describe in detail.
2. When you think about this word, how could it impact you and the relationships in your life? Describe in detail.
3. When you think about this word, what is stopping you from growing in this area of your life? Describe in detail.

Word 2: ANGER

Definition

To make somebody angry

Bible Verse

Get rid of all bitterness, rage, and anger, brawling and slander, along with every form of malice. ~ Ephesians 4:31 NIV

Food for Thought

Anger is an acid that can do more harm to the vessel in which it is stored than to anything on which it is poured. ~Mark Twain

Contemplation

I think the quote from Mark Twain paints a radically real picture of this word anger because anger is a negative emotion. Anger acts like an acid, meaning, it will deteriorate and eat away at the vessel with which it is stored. Unfortunately, for humans, the vessel that anger is stored in is our own selves. It can and will eat away at you and it has the capacity to destroy you.

You also carry inside of you the capacity to harm others when you pour your anger out on other people. It is worth noting that pouring your anger out on other people does not diminish the amount of anger that is inside of you. As a matter of fact, the more you unleash it, the more it actually grows. It grows in both you and the person you are targeting with your anger. Anger is a very powerful negative emotion. Nobody enjoys carrying it within nor do we like to experience it from others. One of the great ways to change the way we live in the world is to understand the destructive power of this word anger. We know that it does not serve us, so how do we begin to get rid of it?

The first thing to do is to recognize that you have it. Recognize that you've probably been building it up for a long period of time. Anger builds up over time much like a volcano builds up over a period of time before it erupts. This can come into view by watching the way you respond to the way someone cuts you off in traffic, or the way you respond to your kids when they are out of control. We have all been triggered with this emotion called anger. Immediately after unleashing your anger, you may say, "Wow, where did that come from?" It can sound and feel like a fire-breathing dragon.

There are a couple of steps you can take to get rid of anger. Step number one is to recognize that is there. The second step is to not judge it. Many people actually create more anger because they are angry that they have anger. Ha! Think of how insane that is. It is not a matter of "right" or "wrong" for having it. Anger is just an emotion do not give it any power over you. Step number three is to let it go and release it's capacity to harm you. One of the primary reasons to let it go is because we are all designed to impact other humans, and to impact other humans in the most beneficial way possible. In order to impact others positively, we need to make sure we are clear of negative emotions like anger. This process of letting go is a personal journey to find the best method for you. Some people like to meditate about it while others like to pray about it. Find a way that works for you and give it time to take hold.

I would like to shine a light on a few more observations about anger. The more this negative emotion called anger builds inside of you as a toxin, the less you are able to utilize your senses. It has the capacity to blur your vision, it has the capacity to deafen your ears, and it also has the capacity to harden your heart. Holding anger, your senses won't be as active and alive as they ought to be. This acid, called anger deteriorates all of your senses.

If you want to become an impact player, lead other people, and become a leader of leaders, then you really owe it to others, to find a way to diminish this negative emotion called anger. As my good friend Blair Singer says, "When your emotions go up, your intelligence goes down." In other words, when your emotions go up, your capacity to see, hear, feel and interact in the world goes down significantly.

∞

Empower Thought

Please take the time and look at the truth of the word anger. Be truthful with yourself and see if you have it somewhere inside of you. Remember to not judge it, just recognize that it's there, and find a way to let it go because I truly believe that when you do that, the way that you live in the world will begin to change. Your ability to help somebody else will greatly increase in its capacity because this acid called anger won't dull your senses.

Questions to Ponder

1. When you think of what is going on in the world, what does this word make you think about? Describe in detail.
2. When you think about this word, how could it impact you and the relationships in your life? Describe in detail.
3. When you think about this word, what is stopping you from growing in this area of your life? Describe in detail.

Word 3: ANXIETY

Definition

Fear or nervousness about what might happen

Bible Verse

Do not be anxious about anything, but in every situation, by prayer and petition with thanksgiving, present your requests to God.
~ Philippians 4:6 NIV

Food for Thought

Nothing diminishes anxiety faster than action. ~ Walter Anderson

Contemplation

Most people experience anxiety when they are thinking about something in the future. Anxiety likes to create "what if" scenarios in your mind that lead to non-optimal thought processes. These thought processes will leave you paralyzed and with the inability to start moving towards a goal. Anxiety is a very real issue.

If we go back to the dictionary definition that says, "fear or nervousness about what might happen". So many people that I have met all over the world create this game called "what if". The game goes like this, "what if this doesn't happen" or "what if that doesn't happen"? Pretty soon, you're thoughts have created a jungle of anxiety built from all these "what if" scenarios. Remember, these thoughts are not about something that's going to happen, but rather, something that "might happen". Therefore, it becomes important to become aware of these "what if" scenarios, these thoughts about things that may or may not occur in the future. Do not allow the negative scenarios to become a story that you tell yourself, because if you build this jungle of anxiety up in front of you, it's going to be very hard for you to try to navigate your way through life every single day. It will begin to look like it there is no clear path and no clear ending.

Why do we allow ourselves to create the jungle of anxiety? One of the pre-dominate reasons is that our thoughts come from our emotions. If you have fear or anxiety or nervousness about something, that's an emotion. That emotion is like an anchor that begins to pull down all kinds of thoughts into it a thought pattern. With a negative emotional anchor like anxiety, what types of thoughts do you think are going to come your way? Do you think positive thoughts are going to come your way, or do you think negative thoughts are going to come your way? If you have a negative anchor, negative thoughts are going to come your way and you're going to get flooded with more negative thoughts, creating a negative thought pattern.

If you're currently sitting in that jungle of anxiety, you need to ask yourself an important question. You need to ask this one question every day for the next seven days in a row. The question is, "What is the number one negative emotion that you're hiding from?" The quickest way to find a path in the jungle of anxiety is to shine a light into the darkness. The moment you can identify the number one negative emotion that you are hiding from, that is the moment that your awareness begins to recognize the pattern. You will recognize that the jungle of anxiety does not serve you and it does not serve others.

Once you can identify it, you will be able to move through a process of letting it go. The process of letting it go can be through prayer or through meditation. You will need to work through the process that supports you the most.

∞

Empower Thought

Think about this word anxiety. Anxiety is built off of fear and nervousness. It's also built off of something that "might happen". Pay attention to see if you're creating this jungle of anxiety for yourself, and if you are, ask yourself one question, "What is the number one emotion that you're hiding from"? I guarantee that if you find it, the jungle is going to be opened up, and you're going to find a path. Think on this word anxiety.

Questions to Ponder

1. When you think of what is going on in the world, what does this word make you think about? Describe in detail.
2. When you think about this word, how could it impact you and the relationships in your life? Describe in detail.
3. When you think about this word, what is stopping you from growing in this area of your life? Describe in detail.

Word 4: ATTITUDE

Definition

The way you think or feel about someone or something

Bible Verse

Do not conform to the pattern of this world, but be transformed by the renewing of your mind. Then you will be able to test and approve what God's will is, His good, pleasing and perfect will. ~ Romans 12:2 NIV

Food for Thought

Attitude is a little thing that makes a big difference. ~ Anonymous

Contemplation

Let's start by looking at the definition of the word attitude, "it's the way that you think or feel". These words, thinking and feeling are two important words that shape your attitude. Which one drives the other? Does your thinking drive your emotions, or do your emotions drive your thinking?

Have you ever heard the phrase "Attitude is everything"? I know that attitude is an extremely important part of the way that you move through the world, but I don't know that it should hold the mantle for "everything". I want to challenge that position with you for just a moment because I believe by doing so, we can tap into a positive source of power. I think that this source of power comes from the awareness that your attitude can take hold of one of two positions. You can have a positive attitude, or you can have a very negative attitude. Most of us have experienced this positive and negative attitude all throughout the day, as a matter of fact, all throughout our life. Obviously we all want to have a more positive attitude, but very often we get trapped by a negative attitude.

So what drives these positive and negative attitudes? Does our thinking drive attitudes, or are they driven by our emotions? In my experience, the one that is the driver is our emotions. There are very powerful positive emotions like love, gratitude, faith, hope, and compassion. Then there are very negative emotions like fear, anxiety, worry, greed, and envy. If left unchecked and unaware, you may be carrying more negative emotions than positive emotions. These emotions can begin to fill up inside of you much like water filling up a container. Everyday, if you have negative emotions going unchecked, that's just making this container bigger and bigger, and pretty soon, you're carrying around this massive load on you of negative emotions. This creates something called your emotional framework. This emotional framework in turn is what drives or attracts your thinking to you. Most of the thoughts you have all day are attracted or driven by your emotions. If you have very negative emotions like fear, worry or anxiety, then most of the day, you'll find that you have negative thoughts. These thoughts just keep coming and coming, ultimately shaping your attitude into a more negative one. The good news is the same process is true for positive emotions, thoughts and attitudes.

∞

Empower Thought

The more you can become aware of your emotional framework, the more aware you become of the power it has to shift your attitude. Attitude is not "everything" since they are anchored to thoughts driven by emotions. Getting to the source of the issue builds internal capacity for you to shift your attitude in the right direction. Power is the awareness of your attitude, shaped by thoughts, driven by emotions both negative and positive. As humans, we are designed with the capacity to become aware of our design and mange that design into the direction that best serves us and other humans.

Questions to Ponder

1. When you think of what is going on in the world, what does this word make you think about? Describe in detail.
2. When you think about this word, how could it impact you and the relationships in your life? Describe in detail.
3. When you think about this word, what is stopping you from growing in this area of your life? Describe in detail.

Word 5: BELIEF

Definition

A feeling of being sure that someone or something exists or that something is true.

Bible Verse

We live by faith, not by sight. ~ 2 Corinthians 5:7 NIV

Food for Thought

A belief is not merely an idea that the mind possesses; it is an idea that possesses the mind. ~ Robert Bolton

Contemplation

Belief is something that's going on in the mind with our trust or our belief in someone or something. We are not just dealing with ourselves here. In the quote above, beliefs come from an idea. This idea or this belief has so much power in it that it can possess our mind. It's not necessarily the mind reaching out and possessing this idea, rather, it's the belief itself that grabs hold of the mind. The idea or belief takes possession of the mind and there, in turn lies the truth, the power of this word, belief. Beliefs come from somewhere else and they can grab hold of us.

Most people will never take the time to pause and reflect on the beliefs that have taken root in their minds. I challenge you to pause now and reflect on your different beliefs. Beliefs you may hold about money, or relationships, or your ability to learn or even beliefs you have about your spiritual life. The moment we are able to separate ourselves and examine ourselves from a third person, we can begin to identify if the beliefs we are holding onto are serving us with our ultimate purpose or calling for our life. Or are these beliefs actually shrinking and diminishing our capacity to fulfill what it is that we're here to do?

If you look close enough you can see the gears of your belief system turning within you. This is called your operating system of beliefs. Picture at least four gears that are turning inside of your mind, much like that of a clock or a machine. When one of the gears turns, they all begin to turn. Every human was designed with this system and the gears of the mind are always turning.

We all hold beliefs about something. It could be a belief about why you're here, your purpose for being here, your passions and your dreams. You have beliefs about relationships. You have beliefs about your financial wellbeing. You also have beliefs about your spiritual life. The longer that your life progresses the longer a set of beliefs can grab hold of you. The longer that belief grabs ahold of you the longer that that gear turns around in your mind, the more that you're going to hold on to this belief. The gears of the operating center of beliefs just keep turning and turning and turning, basically building neural muscle inside your mind. That is how an idea can possess the mind because the more the belief gear turns, the more you hold on to it.

What happens next is that when you get presented with a different option, a different reality, a different belief, a different absolute truth, what's going to happen is, you are going to come face to face with a choice. Stay with this old belief that has been holding onto you for a long period of time or choose to look at a new belief. This new belief that comes in, it may hold more truth in it, but because you've been holding on to an old belief for such a long period of time, it becomes very difficult for you to accept the reality of the truth of this new belief. Even though this new belief may hold more truth in it, you probably will not accept this new belief system because you've been holding this other belief for such a long time, and so you continue to choose the old belief and then your life ultimately gets run by it.

Many people miss out their true calling in life and miss opportunities to pursue it because they never pause and reflect to look at their beliefs. They never examine and see how beliefs have taken a hold of their minds. There is power in the ability to pause, reflect and gain clarity of your belief systems and ultimately your life. One of the ways to do this is by asking yourself a couple of questions regarding your operating center of beliefs.

You begin by identifying 4 or 5 beliefs that have grabbed a hold of you around money, relationships, knowledge and spiritual growth. Then ask yourself the following questions.

- Where did that belief come from?
- Who did I learn this belief from?
- Does this belief serve me or is it stopping me from getting to where I need to go?

∞

Empower Thought

By looking at the truth of this word, belief, we can begin to change the way we live in the world. I challenge you to look objectively and see that your beliefs are moving the gears of your mind like a machine. Remember, the longer you've had those beliefs, the more you're going to hold on to them. The more you hold them, the more you'll choose them and then the more they will run your life. Therefore, you owe it to yourself and you deserve to pause and reflect on this word belief.

Questions to Ponder

1. When you think of what is going on in the world, what does this word make you think about? Describe in detail.
2. When you think about this word, how could it impact you and the relationships in your life? Describe in detail.
3. When you think about this word, what is stopping you from growing in this area of your life? Describe in detail.

Word 6: BLESSING

Definition

Approval that allows or helps you to do something

Bible Verse

Land that drinks in the rain often falling on it, and that produces a crop
useful to those for whom it was farmed, receives a blessing from God.
~ Hebrews 6:7 NIV

Food for Thought

Talk about your blessings more than you talk about your burdens.
~ Anonymous

Contemplation

Burdens can blind your sight but blessings also have the power to awaken your vision. If we started talking about our blessings more than we shared our burdens, I know the way that we live in the world would begin to change. Choosing to focus on your blessings allows you to gain a positive vision or perspective on your life.

Most people have dreams and ambitions for a type of life they would like to have. However, I have seen so many people get trapped in the pursuit of "things". The grind to acquire makes some people feel overly burdened. They experience fear or have anxiety because they don't currently have what they are pursuing. They give away all their power and happiness to a "thing" in the future. Meaning, they have created a scenario where they cannot experience blessings until they acquire something. Then once they acquire the thing, the joy of the blessing is minimal. Starting a whole new cycle of burdens.

You have the power to allow blessings to awaken your vision and happiness. Do not lose sight of all the great things that have occurred and that are occurring in your life. Because most are so focused on something they don't have, you forget to pause and reflect and say you know what, I do have a tremendous amount of blessings that are here right now. And if I can just focus my attention on the blessings that I currently have, that will actually provide me the strength and power and resource that I need in order to get me through the troubles and burdens of getting me to where I'm trying to get to tomorrow. You see our blessings can become the fuel for where we're tying to get to in the future.

So I'd like to share with you a process that I believe, will help you focus on your current blessings and provide you the fuel, give you the capacity, the strength, the perseverance and character to be able to move on and go forward. Grab a notebook and a quite spot to ponder and reflect.

Then ask yourself the following questions.

- What are you most grateful for today?
- Who are you most grateful for today?
- What does somebody else do that you are most grateful for today?
- Make a list of the 10 things you are most grateful for right now.
- What is the vision you have for your life?
- What is the next step you need to take to move towards that vision?

∞

Empower Thought

Go through that exercise, pause and reflect on the questions. I think that you'll be amazed at how many blessings you have. I also believe they will awaken the vision for your life. I am confident that you have a tremendous amount to be thankful for. You have a tremendous amount of blessings. You've been born a living-breathing miracle. Rick Warren, a pastor and author, referenced the fact that you are alive is evidence that your life has a purpose. I know you're trying to get somewhere, but focus on your blessings and they'll give you the strength and the fuel that will take you to where you're trying to get to. Then, the way that you live in the world will begin to change.

Questions to Ponder

1. When you think of what is going on in the world, what does this word make you think about? Describe in detail.
2. When you think about this word, how could it impact you and the relationships in your life? Describe in detail.
3. When you think about this word, what is stopping you from growing in this area of your life? Describe in detail.

Word 7: CHANGE

Definition

To become different or to become something else

Bible Verse

How I wish I could be with you now and change my tone because I'm perplexed about you. ~ Galatians 4:20 NIV

Food for Thought

The secret of change is to focus all of your energy, not on fighting the old but on building the new. ~ Socrates

Contemplation

I think that most people would like to change some part of their life if not all of their life completely. They'd like to change a relationship, they'd like to change a job, and they would like to change what they do for a living. They'd like to change where they live. They'd like to change their appearance. There's a lot of focus around the word "change," yet so many people seem to fail at their ability to create change. Why?

Socrates said, "The secret of change is to focus all of your energy not in fighting the old but on building the new." So often we tend to spend our energy on looking at our past experiences and results, coming away displeased. We may then begin to feel regret, shame, guilt, anger, envy or frustration at what has or has not occurred in our lives. As humans, we spend a lot of unfruitful energy focusing on our past as opposed to putting all of our energy into creating our future.

The past can become your greatest teacher. The past is something to learn from. It holds the keys of opportunity to paint the picture of where you would like to go. It can shape the direction you would like to go and it can shape the trajectory you would like to go. If the secret of change is to focus all of your energy on building the new, then the ability to focus is key.

If focus is key to change, then we need the ability to focus on where we put our energy. A great friend of mine, Kelly Ritchie, always reminds me to become aware of energy flows. How you use your energy and where you focus your energy. He would always remind me that, "Jason, energy always flows and energy always flows to the least line of resistance." If you think about energy in your life, recognize that energy is always flowing. It's much like water. If you were to look at a raging young river, it has the ability to cut through rock. However, over time you recognize that the water tries to find the least line of resistance. The older that a river is the more that it meanders. The more it twists and turns because it's trying to find the least line of resistance. Nature is always trying to do ever more with ever less. The same thing is true for you in your life and that's why it becomes so difficult to change, because your energy is always flowing to the least line of resistance.

For example, if you'd like to get physically fit and change your fitness level, it is going to require you to put your energy into changing. You will need to put energy into getting up earlier. You will need to put energy into going to the gym. You will need to put energy into lifting weights. You will need to put energy into cardio fitness. You will need to put energy into focusing on what kind of food are you going put in your body. You will need to put energy into educating yourself a little bit more. You will need to put energy into being able to do that every single day, of every single week, of every single month, for the rest of your life.

It's not like you only have to put energy into getting physically fit for a week and that's it. That's all you're ever going to have to do. Change requires you to put in energy every single day as a way of life for a long period of time and ultimately people will look at your body and they'll say, "Wow, what did you do to change yourself? You've made such a big change in your life and your physical appearance." What most people don't recognize, or they fail to acknowledge, is the amount of energy that goes into every single day. It is hard to change because you're always hitting against the boundary of your capacity to change. Your dissatisfaction, your willingness and your desire to change must be greater than the resistance to not change. Otherwise, energy is going to flow into the least line of resistance and you're not going to change.

If you've built up a habit of sleeping in, not going to the gym, not lifting weights, not doing cardiovascular exercise, and eating poor foods, then it's going to be very hard for you to change because there's an enormous amount of resistance to change. Change happens in small little building blocks. Change happens in small little disciplines. Change happens in small little commitments. You don't have to change for your entire life. You just have to change for this moment in time. Just right now. You just need your desire and energy to change to be greater than the resistance not to change. Just for today.

∞

Empower Thought

Tell yourself - today I'm going to lift weights. Today, I'm going to go for a walk. Today, I'm going to eat a little bit healthier. That's all you have to do today. Then wake up tomorrow and you're going to say the same thing. Just for today, I'm going to move my body and just for today, I'm going to eat right. You will begin to recognize that change is nothing more than small little disciplines and small little commitments. You will end up where you want to go – changed for the better!

Questions to Ponder

1. When you think of what is going on in the world, what does this word make you think about? Describe in detail.
2. When you think about this word, how could it impact you and the relationships in your life? Describe in detail.
3. When you think about this word, what is stopping you from growing in this area of your life? Describe in detail.

Word 8: COMMITMENT

Definition

A promise to do or give something, a promise to be loyal to someone or something

Bible Verse

Commit to the Lord whatever you do, and he will establish your plans.
~ Proverbs 16:3 NIV

Food for Thought

Most people are committed to a lack of commitment. ~ Jeffrey Benjamin

Contemplation

Commitment is a promise to do or give something, it's a promise to be loyal, and it's an agreement or pledge to do something in the future. The word "promise" shows up two times and it also uses the word "agreement". These are key words that provide clues to understand our word of commitment. For most of us, once we make a commitment it's often very difficult to keep it.

The ability to keep a commitment is an equal opportunity employer for both large and small commitments that we make. I am sure we can all relate to breaking small commitments like showing up somewhere on time, responding to an email or returning a phone call. Even harder to keep commitments are the ones that involve a week, month, year, decade or a lifetime. Large commitments like to a marriage, or to your children, or to a business partner, or to your health, or to quit drinking, or quit smoking. These are commitments that we all make to ourselves during the course of life, and sometimes they're very, very difficult to keep.

This is also true for commitments we make to ourselves or to other people. The inability to keep a commitment to others shrinks our capacity to get things done and to be able to achieve the things we want to and it hinders our growth in all areas of our lives. Why?

One of the reasons we lack the capacity to keep a commitment is because it is so easy to quit. You have to build the capacity to *defy the urge to quit*. Most people are bad judges of distance. Let me give you an example of a bad judge of distance. Let's say you are here today and you want something in the future. So you make a commitment to yourself or to somebody else that you're going to move from here and you're ultimately going to get to over there in the future. From this point today to that point tomorrow, there's a distance. Most people are bad at judging the distance and most people are bad at navigating the journey from here to there. Most forget to realize that the journey from here to there is a daily discipline.

Commitment is a daily discipline. Commitment is a bridge that builds you from today to the next day, to the next day, to the next and so on until you are there. Commitment is built over time. Every single day you need to be committed to the agreement or promise that you made that will ultimately get you there.

Time is going to keep moving, so while you're moving through time, you just have to stay committed at every point in time. So every hour, of every day, of every week, of every month, of every year, you just need to be committed, but it all starts just being committed every single moment.

If you can stay committed for one day, you can stay committed for two days. And if you can stay committed for two days, you've already proven that you can stay committed for three. And if you can stay committed for three, you can stay committed for four, and ultimately five, six, and seven. Then you've already proven that you can stay committed for a week, which then means you can stay committed for two weeks, and then three weeks, and then four weeks, and then you've proven that you can stay committed for a month, which ultimately will lead you into a year.

∞

Empower Thought

With this word "commitment" I challenge you to just stay committed for a day. That will ultimately become a small little building block that will build into a week that will build into a month that will ultimately build into a year, and hopefully into a decade, and ultimately for the rest of your life. This ability will change the way you live in the world. It's a powerful word that has a ton of truth built inside of it, but it requires these small little steps of commitment just every single day. Don't forget to defy the urge to quit with this word commitment.

Questions to Ponder

1. When you think of what is going on in the world, what does this word make you think about? Describe in detail.
2. When you think about this word, how could it impact you and the relationships in your life? Describe in detail.
3. When you think about this word, what is stopping you from growing in this area of your life? Describe in detail.

Word 9: COMPASSION

Definition

A sympathetic consciousness of others distress together with a desire to alleviate it.

Bible Verse

Therefore, as God's chosen people, holy and dearly loved, clothe yourselves with compassion. ~ Colossians 3:12 NIV

Food for Thought

Compassion is a necessity not a luxury. ~ Dalai Lama

Contemplation

Regardless of where you live in the world or how you've been raised, compassion is an important word. The way that the dictionary defines compassion is extremely important. It is a sympathetic consciousness, in other words, it is an awareness of other people's distress, their troubles, their anxieties, and their fears. Having an awareness of other people's fears, anxieties or worries, together with a desire from you to alleviate it.

There is a huge difference between compassion acted out as a noun and compassion acted out as a verb. Compassion acted out as a noun, merely means that you are aware of other people's problems and distresses. That's a great ability to have. The ability to recognize that in the world people have fears, anxieties, hunger, pollution, relational and spiritual problems. Everybody has problems. The ability to be aware of other people's problems and have some form of compassion for them is a great starting part. That is compassion as a noun, awareness with no action required.

I'd like to challenge you to move towards compassion as a verb. Compassion as a verb means that once you become aware of the problems, you actually are compelled to do something about it. It's like the definition says "…together with a desire to alleviate it". It stirs up something inside of you that says being aware of other people's problems isn't good enough for me. Now that I'm aware of other people's problems, I actually need to be a catalyst or a driver to create a condition to solve or alleviate those problems. It compels you to move, it compels you to act, and it compels you to do something. It creates a passion inside of you so intense that you turn your passion into action. You make the shift from knowing that something exists to actually doing something about it.

∞

Empower Thought

Most people like to complain or point fingers as to why a problem in the world exists. It takes courage and it takes someone with leadership to actually recognize the problem and then move towards doing something about it. Through this process of looking at the word of compassion, I'd like for you to challenge yourself to move towards action. Shift into motion towards wanting to alleviate it. Not for your benefit, but for the benefit of somebody else. The challenge is learning to walk through the world with compassion, realizing that compassion is a necessity and it's not just a luxury.

Questions to Ponder

1. When you think of what is going on in the world, what does this word make you think about? Describe in detail.
2. When you think about this word, how could it impact you and the relationships in your life? Describe in detail.
3. When you think about this word, what is stopping you from growing in this area of your life? Describe in detail.

Word 10: CONNECTION

Definition

Something that joins or connects two or more things together

Bible Verse

And in Christ you are being built together becoming a holy temple for the Lord. ~ Ephesians 2:22 NIV

Food for Thought

A hidden connection is stronger than an obvious one. ~ Heraclitus of Ephesus

Contemplation

The statement that a hidden connection is stronger than an obvious one sheds light onto a quality about the word connection. It is a quality that is unseen or invisible and at the same time, extremely powerful. If we go to the dictionary definition, it says to connect "...two or more things" often with the same cause, origin, or goal. So this invisible quality of the word connection is related to the intention of being connected.

Connection allows harmony and connection allows rhythm. Connection can also allow for increased stability between two or more things being connected. We've all experienced feelings of being able to connect with someone, something or somewhere. You meet somebody for the first time and you feel like you have an instant connection with him or her. Or you go someplace new and you feel like you have an instant connection with that place. Maybe you really love being at the beach, or in a big city, or on a boat in the middle of a lake, or up in the mountains.

Wherever it is, you have an immediate connection with it and you know it. Or maybe you have a connection to a group of people in your neighborhood, the gym or your church.

Connections allow for strong human-to-human bonds to form. To begin to understand this powerful design between you and others, it will be beneficial to ask yourself some questions. By asking questions, you will begin to create awareness as to why connections are important to you. Ask yourself the following questions, "Why do I feel good when I'm with this person?" or "Why do I feel good when I'm in this environment?"

In other words, when you're connected to someone or something that is true for you, you're in harmony with it. When you're connected with things that make you feel good, it provides a certain rhythm to you. You feel less stress. You feel more alive. Your senses are more in tune. It also provides stability for you. If you go to a place where you feel well connected, the chaos of the world seems to quiet down and move away. This becomes a powerful anchor for those moments in life where you begin to feel dis-connected.

We all have this urge to feel connected to other people. It's an invisible desire that comes from somewhere. This desire to be connected is trying to lead us in a direction, but where and for what purpose? I believe your life has a significant purpose and when you get connected with other like-minded humans, together, you create a harmony that has the potential to create infinite possibilities. The key questions to ask are:

- What are you getting connected to?
- What is the reason you want to get connected to that?
- Who is it that you need to be connected to?
- What is something bigger than yourself that you need to get connected to, and if you did, would provide harmony, rhythm, and stability for you?
- What is something big that is out there?

∞

Empower Thought

I think that all of us know we want to be connected to something bigger than ourselves. And if you could connect to something bigger than yourself, it would ultimately provide the stability that you're looking for in your life. That is significant because it will provide the opportunity for you to change the way that you live in the world.

Questions to Ponder

1. When you think of what is going on in the world, what does this word make you think about? Describe in detail.
2. When you think about this word, how could it impact you and the relationships in your life? Describe in detail.
3. When you think about this word, what is stopping you from growing in this area of your life? Describe in detail.

Word 11: COURAGE

Definition

The ability to do something that you know is difficult or dangerous.

Bible Verse

Be strong and courageous. Do not be afraid or terrified because of them, because the Lord your God goes with you, and He will never leave you nor forsake you. ~ Deuteronomy 6 NIV

Food for Thought

With courage you will dare to take risks, have the strength to be compassionate, and wisdom to be humble. Courage is the foundation of integrity. ~ Mark Twain

Contemplation

Courage is the ability to do something that you know is difficult or dangerous. Where does the ability to have courage come from? Most of us would love to believe that we have to have all the courage inside of us to face our challenges and fears in life. In my experience, that will only get you so far, but you'll never reach your full capacity.

A great opportunity to grow through this word courage is the moment you can realize courage is also about having the strength to trust others to support you. It takes courage to have trust and faith in someone else. It takes courage to have trust and faith in something much bigger than you. Anybody can muster up enough courage inside of himself or herself for a short while, however, very few people actually have the awareness to recognize how powerful it could be to have courage in somebody else or to trust in something bigger than you.

If you could develop the ability to trust others to support you, you would begin to realize that things would change all around you. You'll be able to see things that you've never seen, opportunities that you never knew existed. You'll be able to hear things that you've never heard before. You'll be able to move through the world in a totally different way because you will be able to venture, you will able to persevere, you will dare to take risks, have the strength to be compassionate, and the wisdom to be humble.

∞

Empower Thought

I know that it's tough a challenge. Most people, when you tell them to have courage, faith and trust in others, that somehow, that becomes dis-encouraging for them. However, if you're able to move through that process, you'll recognize that it's not discouraging to do those things. Rather, it becomes very encouraging. You'll recognize other people are willing and able to support you. You'll recognize opportunities will open up. You'll also recognize that some of the difficulties will seem to dissipate and begin to fade away.

Questions to Ponder

1. When you think of what is going on in the world, what does this word make you think about? Describe in detail.
2. When you think about this word, how could it impact you and the relationships in your life? Describe in detail.
3. When you think about this word, what is stopping you from growing in this area of your life? Describe in detail.

Word 12: DEATH

Definition

The end of life, a time when someone or something dies, the permanent end of something

Bible Verse

For the wages of sin is death, but the Gift of God is eternal life in Jesus Christ our Lord.. ~ Romans 6:23 NIV

Food for Thought

The day of my birth, me death began its walk. It is walking towards me without hurrying. ~ Jean Cocteau

Contemplation

Death means the "permanent end of something." Some people think of this word death as a morbid, sad and dark word. I find that most people are afraid of death and afraid of dying. The primary reason is because so many people are unsure about what is truly on the other side of death. That uncertainty creates fear, worry and confusion.

As humans we have the unique opportunity to observe and experience life, as well as, observe and experience death. Whether it is the death of a loved one, death of a friend, death of a family member, we hear of death, or we see death. We get to observe humans being born and we get to witness humans dying. We see animals born and we see animals die, we see trees grow and we see trees die. We get to witness the whole process that takes place, beginning to end. While some view this process disturbing, I believe there is so much value in trying to look at death with the proper perspective.

This perspective can start with a process of life called a gestation period. From the time that a seed is planted to the time that it starts to grow, that's called the gestation period. The same thing is true for us as humans; we are born from a seed inside our mother's womb. There is a gestation period when you're growing inside of your mother's womb to ultimately being born out into the world. All living things have this gestation period, from the moment of the seed until the moment of birth. Then a new gestation period begins which is from the moment of birth until the moment of physical death.

The big question then becomes, what happens at the moment of physical death? Is it the permanent end of something and/or is it the beginning of something new? That questions fires off an internal battle between your ego and your spirit. Everybody has this battle between the ego and your spirit. I believe when you get clarity with your spirit, which is your real purpose for being born; it will open up a new gestation period for you. This time however, with your spiritual growth, you may begin to recognize that God has something greater in store for you after your physical body dies. That gift, if recognized, will be the moment that your spiritual life will begin and your true calling for eternity begins.

One thing that is certain is that we're all going to die a physical death at some moment in time. The ability to face this radical reality can allow for real growth to happen for you. It allows us an opportunity to pause and reflect and think about life as we think about this word called death. Death for me, and the way that I would challenge you to think about it today, is that it actually means life. Death means that you're actually alive. If you can have a conversation about it, it means you have an opportunity to change the way that you live in the world. It starts with the question of why were you born in the first place?

∞

Empower Thought

I think that that's a great opportunity for us to grow. There is hidden capacity that sits inside of all of us. I think that we have infinite potentiality if we choose to look at death as an opportunity to look, ponder and grow our spiritual lives. We know that death is going to come knocking at the door. We do not know the time and we do not know the place. Therefore, during the process of life, it holds the uniqueness of leading us to a new life after physical death. Just like if you see a leaf on a tree that dies off and falls to the ground, well, that leaf becomes dirt that allows for new life to begin. I think the same thing with your life; the process of decay actually leads to a process of new life.

Questions to Ponder

1. When you think of what is going on in the world, what does this word make you think about? Describe in detail.
2. When you think about this word, how could it impact you and the relationships in your life? Describe in detail.
3. When you think about this word, what is stopping you from growing in this area of your life? Describe in detail.

Word 13: EGO

Definition

The opinion that you have of yourself, especially contrasted with another self or the world.

Bible Verse

I can do nothing on my own. As I hear, I judge, and my judgment is just because I seek not my own will but the will of Him who sent me.
~ John 5:30 NIV

Food for Thought

Ego is just like dust in the eye. Without clearing the dust, you can't see anything clearly. So, clear the ego, and see the world. ~ Anonymous

Contemplation

My experience in working with people all over this world has made me aware that every human is in a constant battle every single day of their lives. This constant battle is between our ego and our spirit. Starting with the dictionary definition of the word ego, it says, "an opinion that you have of yourself, especially contrasted or compared to another self". The battle is internal and it is also external. It is an internal battle against our own spirit and it is an external battle because we compare ourselves to others.

Is your ego getting in the way of your spirit growing? Your ego can get in the way, "it can be like dust in the eye that doesn't allow for you see things clearly". Real internal growth comes when we can get real about this battle. The ego was designed originally to protect you from danger, as a survival mechanism. However, over time, it begins to build a wall between you and your spirit. You begin to pay less and less attention to your spirit, your hopes, your dreams, your passions and your real purpose for living. A part of you slowly starts to die inside. You have the capacity to reverse the tide and live more from your spirit.

Left unchecked, you can fall into a second battle with the ego. This is the external battle of comparing yourself to others. We all can fall into this trap with the ego. The ego moves you into a position where you begin to judge yourself, especially comparing yourself to other people. In doing so, your ego can win the battle called the comparison trap. Pay attention to your current thoughts and emotions that are dominating your conversations, your views of the world and your relationships with other people. Do you want to be seen as more successful than somebody else? Do you want to be seen as a success? Do you want to be seen as strong? Do you want to be right in all your conversations? If so, your ego is driving the self-image you have of yourself.

Be careful, because your ego can and will justify your positions, and it will justify decisions that you've made. It will justify why you've done the things that you've done, the decisions that you've made and the circumstances that you find yourself in. This actually takes away your power to become the type of person that you're spirit truly deserves. We've all experienced this. We've all compared ourselves to somebody else. We have all had periods of time where we have pursued opportunities because of greed or personal gain. We've all been envious of somebody else at some moment in our lives. My hope is that you begin to recognize that the ego, in this respect, does not serve you. It's not serving you to be greedy. It's not serving you to be envious. It doesn't serve you to want to compete with somebody else. It doesn't serve you to compare yourself to somebody else. It doesn't serve you to judge other people.

∞

Empower Thought

There is an opportunity for real growth here if we can get the dust of the ego out of our eyes to see clearly. We can start today by answering a couple of questions.

- How have I been driven by my ego?
- Am I being more driven by my ego or am I being more driven by my spirit?
- Am I more driven by economic gains or spiritual growth?

The way we live in the world will change for the better the moment we can begin to trust our spirit more than our ego.

Questions to Ponder

1. When you think of what is going on in the world, what does this word make you think about? Describe in detail.
2. When you think about this word, how could it impact you and the relationships in your life? Describe in detail.
3. When you think about this word, what is stopping you from growing in this area of your life? Describe in detail.

Word 14: ETERNITY

Definition

A time without end, a state that comes after death and never ends.

Bible Verse

I will give them eternal life, and they shall never perish. No one will snatch them out of my hand. ~ John 10:28 NIV

Food for Thought

What we do in life echoes in all of eternity. ~ Anonymous

Contemplation

All civilizations, all throughout the world, regardless of country, race, or religion, all humans recognize that we all have a disease, and the disease is called mortality. There is a 100% guarantee that all humans will die at some moment in their life. Every second, 3 people pass away. Almost 180 people die every minute of every day. That means that every hour approximately 11,000 people die. Every single day, there are almost 250,000 people that will die. One of these days, you will be included in that number.

I don't share these statistics in way to paint a dark picture of humanity. I share this information for us to contemplate radical reality, so that the way that we live in the world can begin to change. I think that one of the greatest things you could ever do to change the way that you live in the world is to contemplate what this word eternity is going to mean for you and the way you live your life.

When it comes to understanding eternity, whom are you going to listen to? Where will you find sound advice? Where will you find some clues? Where can we find a treasure map of what eternity is going to look like? Eternity is hard to get our arms wrapped around because we don't have anything to compare it to in our lifetime.

We can recognize what a second is. We can recognize that minutes come and minutes go. We can recognize that hours come and hours go. We can recognize that days come and days go. We can recognize that week's come and that weeks go and that months come and months go and that years come and years go. We can count the years that we've been alive, and so we can gauge our moments in time over our life.

However, the challenge comes when you try to take what we know to be true about time and put it up against the backdrop of something that will last forever. For some people, that is the scariest and most fearful thing that they could think of. For other people, it produces great joy and great excitement. A third group of people, just completely checkout, since eternity can be a confusing subject.

I want to challenge you to pause and contemplate that there will be a moment in time that you're going to die. There will be a state that happens from the moment that you die, into this other moment called eternity. I want you to have thought about it, because the way that you live in the world will significantly change when you begin to contemplate eternity. What you do in your life will echo into all of eternity, and so I want to challenge you in your ability to see and recognize the transformation of your life against the backdrop and the trajectory of all of eternity.

How far of a vision do you have for your life? Does your vision only take you to a year or 2 years or 5 years or 10 years into your future? Can you see clearly your entire life inclusive of all of eternity? How far does your vision go, and what is the trajectory of that vision for yourself? In the current way that you're growing your capacity, is it putting you in an upward or downward trajectory for all of eternity? I know it's a big idea. I know it's something that's hard to grasp, but you owe it to your spirit to get it right.

∞

Empower Thought

Eternity is a tough concept to understand because we have nothing to compare it to. It comes with a lot of faith, a lot of hope, and a lot of trust. You owe it to your spirit to find the real truth about eternity. You need to find that for yourself. It will define your purpose for being born. It will define the passions and skills and talents that you have. It'll create a vision of forever for you, and it will set you on a direction and a trajectory of eternity. I hope you can begin to see your life against the backdrop of eternity. Not a year, not five years, not 10 years, not and when you get to retirement age, but forever!

Questions to Ponder

1. When you think of what is going on in the world, what does this word make you think about? Describe in detail.
2. When you think about this word, how could it impact you and the relationships in your life? Describe in detail.
3. When you think about this word, what is stopping you from growing in this area of your life? Describe in detail.

Word 15: FAITH

Definition

A strong belief in someone or something

Bible Verse

Now faith is confidence in what we hope for, and assurance in what we do not see. ~ Hebrews 1:1 NIV

Food for Thought

The weakest part of my life can become the strongest part of my faith.
~ Anonymous

Contemplation

As humans, it is undeniable that we all have areas in our life that are weak. We all have challenges in different areas of our lives. The challenge during these low moments of life is to realize that they can ultimately be the moments that build you up and that they can also be the moments that provide strength for you. These moments in time may be the exact conditions necessary for your faith to grow and mature inside of you.

Sometimes when you're in a deep valley and things are going wrong, somebody comes along to help you out. At just the right time, they provide the resources to get you through a rough patch in your life. It's in those times of despair, anxiety, fear and worry where the seeds of greatness get sown the deepest. Often times when you're going through a struggle, it becomes the opportunity that creates perseverance inside of you. It may also allow you to recognize your capacity to have faith. The capacity to have a faith so great that it will allow you to pick yourself up and dust yourself off.

This is a very powerful word, faith. Faith is such a fundamental building block to the way that we live in the world. Take sitting in a chair as an example. In order to not be concerned with sitting in a chair, I have to have faith in gravity. If I were try and explain what gravity is though, the full scientific definition of it, you'd be blown away. Your mind would melt, you would become confused and quite frankly, you'd get bored and say, "Who cares?" Well you would care if every time you sat in a chair, it fell over. You would begin to wonder, why does this chair fall over every time I go to sit down? Why is it that I always end up on my back? After a while, you would begin to realize that you have no faith in the chair or gravity.

That example is aimed at making you aware that faith is built up over time through tiny little building blocks. You have had the experience of sitting in a chair so many times over the course of your life that you don't even think about gravity when you go to sit down. You do not ask, "Will this chair hold me and is gravity going to cooperate this time?" From experience, you know the chair will hold you up and you know that the chair will stay connected to the ground because of something called gravity. You have faith in it. You can't really see it, but you know that it's there because you've experienced it.

The same thing is true for faith. Faith is like dropping a rock into water. If you dropped a rock into water, the rock is moving downward because of gravity. As soon as the rock hits the water it begins to slow down before it hits the bottom of the water floor. But something interesting happens to the water. As soon as the rock hits the water the energy from the rock dropping, makes the water spread out across the top of the water and this is what we call a ripple effect.

∞

Empower Thought

The more faith you have and the more times you rely on your faith in someone or something bigger than yourself, it's like allowing these ripple effects to go out in your life. The main point is to pay attention at the direction and impact of those ripples. As your faith grows, you'll recognize everything around you begins to change. Notice that your faith will begin to show ripples of success, ripples of trust, ripples of reliability, ripples of perseverance, and ripples of strength. Soon your faith will allow you to see things you have never seen, to hear things you have never heard and to feel things that you have never felt. Ultimately, the way that you live in the world will begin to change.

Questions to Ponder

1. When you think of what is going on in the world, what does this word make you think about? Describe in detail.
2. When you think about this word, how could it impact you and the relationships in your life? Describe in detail.
3. When you think about this word, what is stopping you from growing in this area of your life? Describe in detail.

Word 16: FAMILY

Definition

A group of people who are related to each other, united by certain convictions or a common affiliation

Bible Verse

Be devoted to one another in love and honor one another above yourselves. ~ Romans 12:10 NIV

Food for Thought

It doesn't matter the story we are telling, we're telling the story of family. ~ Erica Lorraine Scheidt

Contemplation

For most, family feels good. Some will say there are problems within a family or you don't get to choose your relatives, but you can choose your friends. That is true, but I also believe there is great power in this word family. Family is a group that allows real unconditional love to be learned, felt, given, and received. In other words, the flow of energy is circular in nature, giving and receiving.

Family offers us an opportunity to feel and experience unconditional love. You are born into a family. If you are a parent, you will have experienced that moment when your child came into this world. That miraculous moment produces within us something that is pure, unconditional love. There are no conditions on that emotion, its just pure joy - pure love. Whether you have children or not, family is a life experience of being bound together with a group of people to move through life with.

46

Life is going to give you ups and life's going to give you downs. Riding the wave of life means that sometimes the waves of life will be rough and sometimes the waves of life will be smooth. But nonetheless, it is more powerful to move through life with a family. They can support you in the bad times and celebrate with you in the good times. For most, family will always be there because the love is unconditional.

Family is a real story that is being told through multiple generations and over thousands of years. Your story, your family story, is currently connected to so many other family stories from the past. If you look back at your family tree and connect all the way back, you will see many branches growing off in multiple directions. The further back you go, the more divisions you will see.

If you had the ability to go all the way back to the beginning of time, you would recognize that there's a story that's being told since the very first humans were here. The story that is being told is what your family did, what they believed, their values, their hopes, their dreams, and their experiences. This journey over thousands of years that led to your birth and opportunity for life.

We would all benefit from a brief pause to contemplate our family's past, present and future. I hope that you recognize that your family's story has been told and will continue to be told for a long, long time. I challenge you to take a long view of your family and of your family's story. There are so many people involved that have produced this moment in time of you being you.

∞

Empower Thought

What are the values, what are the truths, what are the ideas, what is it that you hope for as you look into the future of your family? You have an opportunity to look at the real truth of this word family. You have the opportunity to infuse into your family, for generations to come, unconditional love and a strong value system. Who you are, why are you here, what is your purpose, what is your past, what is your present, and ultimately, what is your future? And you have the ability to shape generations to come in your family. That is why there is power in this word called family. It's a group of people united by certain convictions, and to me the strongest is unconditional love.

Questions to Ponder

1. When you think of what is going on in the world, what does this word make you think about? Describe in detail.
2. When you think about this word, how could it impact you and the relationships in your life? Describe in detail.
3. When you think about this word, what is stopping you from growing in this area of your life? Describe in detail.

Word 17: FEAR

Definition

To be afraid of someone or something, to expect or worry about someone or something

Bible Verse

There is no fear in love but perfect love drives out fear because fear has to do with punishment. The one who fears is not made perfect in love.
~ 1 John 4:18 NIV

Food for Thought

Don't let your fear of what could happen make nothing happen.
~ Anonymous

Contemplation

Fear can be an absolute paralyzer for your life. Sometimes we experience it every day and sometimes we experience it more than others. We all experience fear and you can bet we will all continue to experience fear at moments in our life. However, by understanding the word fear, we can begin to loosen its grip on our lives.

If we look at the dictionary definition, it says, "to be afraid of something or someone," and it also says, "to expect or worry," which means it hasn't arrived yet. Did you get that? It means it hasn't arrived yet. What we are worried about is something that may or may not happen in the future. Many people say that fear is an acronym that stands for False Evidence Appearing Real. There's a lot of truth in that acronym because so many times in life we create beliefs and ideas of something that's going to occur to us. These false beliefs end up creating a bigger pile of fear, which in turn, creates the opposite emotions that serve you. The problem is this false belief structure, dictated by fear, greatly shrinks our capacity to impact our life positively. It also diminishes our ability to serve humanity in a way that we're designed to serve humanity.

Fear is the great paralyzer. It basically stops us dead in our tracks because we become so afraid of what might happen that we don't do anything. Fear is the great paralyzer because it creates so many unknowns. Step one in battling fear is to try and figure out what is it that I don't know? What do I need to know, and where would I go to find the absolute truth of what I need to know? Battling fear requires us to get on offense not defense. We've got to be able to unlock and unleash these barriers that are paralyzing us, that are keeping something unknown to us about who we are and where we come from, and our purpose and our passion for being here. We've got to be able to break those walls down.

I am sure you can recall your experience as a kid around Halloween when you went into a haunted house. As you're walking through this dark maze, there's a lot of fear because there's a lot of darkness. Usually where there's a lot of darkness there's a lot of fear because the darkness creates an environment of unknowns. The darkness and the fear of the unknown beasts around the corner, basically paralyzes you into a very slow walk. As you're walking through this maze of a haunted house, you're moving really slow and you're probably in a crouching position holding onto to somebody else because you don't know what's around the next corner. However, if you were to turn the lights on, you wouldn't be as afraid because you could see around the corner. You could see what's coming up, and all of a sudden things would become known to you. When we're in fear, we have to make it an absolute must that we get to the light. We've got to get to what is true and what is known and what can we rely on in order to shine a light into the darkness. It's like being in a car at nighttime; your car has headlights but you can only see as far as the headlights can go. Even though you cannot see everything, the headlights shine a light on your next step on the journey, and so the same is true for our life. We have to learn to trust the light so that it can break away the paralyzing nature of fear.

∞

Empower Thought

I hope you take the time to look at this word fear today, and ask yourself what is the darkness that's creating the unknowns for you in your life? What could you unlock? What kind of truth could you get to around love and light that all of a sudden would break out and allow you to live in the world differently?

Questions to Ponder

1. When you think of what is going on in the world, what does this word make you think about? Describe in detail.
2. When you think about this word, how could it impact you and the relationships in your life? Describe in detail.
3. When you think about this word, what is stopping you from growing in this area of your life? Describe in detail.

Word 18: FOCUS

Definition

The subject upon which people's attention is focused

Bible Verse

Set your affection on things above, not on things in the earth.
~ Colossians 3:2 NIV

Food for Thought

Always remember, your focus determines your reality. ~ George Lucas

Contemplation

Are you challenged with the ability to focus? Do you struggle with the ability to focus your attention and stay focused for a long period of time? Many of us in this hyper-saturated world can lose our focus every single minute of every single hour of every single day. The ability to focus and stay focused will greatly impact the way you live in the world.

If you had an opportunity to sit back and watch your life play out in a movie theater, what would you notice about your ability to focus? Your life plays out against the backdrop of history just as a movie is played out scene by scene. What would you want the movie of your life to highlight or focus on? Now rewind the movie back to today, and begin to focus your attention on the activities that will produce that vision.

Focus is the capacity to see a clear image, unfortunately, most people never take the time to focus their life. Most people will never adjust the lens of their life and focus it in. What is the clear image that you're trying to create for your life? Do you focus more on positive things or do you focus more on negative things?

I would like to challenge you to think of this word focus in the following categories, length, width, depth, timing and direction.

- **Length:** What is the length of your focus? Can you focus the lens of your life for a day, a week, a month, a year, 5 years, 20 years, your entire lifetime, or eternity?
- **Width:** How wide is your focus? Can you focus only on your life or can you focus on your family's life as well? Can you focus on your neighborhood, your community, your city, your state, your region, your country, your continent, or the world?
- **Depth:** How deep can you focus? Once you understand your unique talents, how deep are you willing to go in order to become an expert in your field? Will you research, read, contemplate, study, share, educate, write, communicate and lead others?
- **Timing:** What is the timing of your focus? How long does it take you to realize that your life is out of focus? Once you realize that you are out of focus, how long does it take you to get back into focus?
- **Direction:** What direction do you want the focus of your life to go? Do you focus more on material things or do you focus more on spiritual things? Do you focus on yesterday or do you focus on tomorrow?

∞

Empower Thought

Always remember that your focus determines your reality. You have the ability to put your attention and adjust the lens of your life. Get a clear image of what you want the movie of your life to focus in on. I hope that you take the time to do that, and I know the way that you live in the world will begin to change.

Questions to Ponder

1. When you think of what is going on in the world, what does this word make you think about? Describe in detail.

2. When you think about this word, how could it impact you and the relationships in your life? Describe in detail.
3. When you think about this word, what is stopping you from growing in this area of your life? Describe in detail.

Word 19: FORGIVENESS

Definition

The act of forgiving someone or something; the attitude of someone who is willing to forgive other people

Bible Verse

All the prophets testify about him, that everyone who believes in him receives forgiveness of sins through his name. ~ Acts 10:43 NIV

Food for Thought

Forgiveness is giving up your right to get even. ~ Anonymous

Contemplation

Have you ever wanted to get even with somebody that you felt wronged you in some way? Are you willing to forgive? Or, do you want to increase your capacity to forgive? This word, forgiveness, is rich with opportunity to grow and change the way we live in the world.

Let's start with the dictionary definition that says forgiveness is "the attitude of someone who is willing to forgive other people." The key word there is "willing". Real growth comes from our willingness to forgive someone that's done something to us or to somebody that we know. We all have a slight tendency towards revenge, an eye for an eye, and a tooth for a tooth. We often feel that we have the right to be able to get even with somebody. It could be in sports, business or in personal relationships. It seems as though we should be justified in attacking back.

The opportunity for growth happens the moment right after the attack. That next moment, when all our emotions go raging up, that is the time to pause and become aware of our capacity to forgive. There is a big difference between being capable of forgiving and having the capacity to forgive. Do you have the capacity or willingness to forgive at the moment of impact?

Let's assumes that someone has done something to you that affected you negatively, and you feel like you ought to get revenge on that person. Often times, in that moment of impact, we want to fight back and get revenge for it, but the other thing that we do is we start to tell other people about it. The reason we turn to others is so we can build a case for why the justification is there to do something back to the person. We are looking for reasons to get revenge instead of reasons to forgive.

So we build up this story inside of our mind, this negative emotional story that actually increases anger and it also increases the need for revenge. You look to others that agree with your side of the story. This process provides the necessary fuel in your tanks to continue the fight, but in reality, you haven't solved anything or created a viable solution.

I challenge you to not fight back at the moment of impact. I challenge you to pause and see it as an opportunity to look and actually see the other individual and have compassion for them. After all, they too are a living-breathing miracle called a human. It's an opportunity to forgive that individual for something that has occurred. It's an opportunity to look at all the different conditions that were there that allowed this type of behavior to come up from both individuals.

∞

Empower Thought

When this situation occurs next time, ask the following questions. What have I learned in this scenario? What is the mature thing for me to do? What's the most loving thing for me to do? What's the most compassionate thing for me to do? It's to forgive the other person, because they, too, may be in a scenario or a condition that they haven't had the opportunity to grow and mature yet. You can become a catalyst, one, to grow yourself, but you can also become a catalyst to grow the other person. What a powerful behavior to create in the world, and it comes with this willingness to forgive.

Questions to Ponder

1. When you think of what is going on in the world, what does this word make you think about? Describe in detail.
2. When you think about this word, how could it impact you and the relationships in your life? Describe in detail.
3. When you think about this word, what is stopping you from growing in this area of your life? Describe in detail.

Word 20: FRIENDS

Definition

A person who you like and enjoy being with

Bible Verse

Greater love has no one than this, to lay down one's life for one's friend.
~ John 15:13 NIV

Food for Thought

Good friends are the sunshine of life. ~ John Hay

Contemplation

Do you believe that friends are the sunshine of life? When I think about things that need sunshine, I think about plants and I think about how the sun provides something that allows the plants to grow. I believe that friends have the capacity to do the same thing for us as humans. When you're together with a friend in conversation, you have the capacity to add richness to each other. This richness can become the foundation for tremendous growth.

I believe that all humans were designed to communicate. We were designed to communicate and share with others our truth, affections, emotions, ideas, joys, dreams and pains. Friends are those people that will walk through life together with us. Friends share a common bond as we experience life. We may not be in the same life situations every single day as our friends, but there's something comforting about a friend and that is why we have them around. Typically, we share a common view of the world that draws us together.

We all need somebody to be on the walk through life together with you. You need somebody to inspire you. You need somebody to motivate you. You need somebody to pick you up and dust you off when you're down on the ground. You need somebody to challenge you. You need somebody to be real with you. You need somebody to cry with. You need somebody that can give you a hug. You need somebody that can just sit and have a conversation with you.

Two is better than one. When two people go out into the world with a common purpose, magical things can begin to happen. I challenge you to build friendships with people that aspire to do the similar thing with you. I challenge you to develop strong bonds of friendship with another person because together, you may be able to impact, teach and educate other humans for the good.

∞

Empower Thought

Friendship is a form of real wealth. Friends are people you can count on. Friends are someone that will hold your arm as you go into the battlefield of life. When you open yourself up to a friend, it allows a real opportunity for you to increase your capacity, to increase your effectiveness, and be able to impact all of humanity in a very positive way. Do you invest into friends as if they are a form of wealth? Do you value friendship as much as you should? The bond of a true friendship should be able to weather any storm. This bond of friendship is the invisibility quality that infuses our sense of worth and can fuel our purpose for living. Friends are the sunshine of life.

Questions to Ponder

1. When you think of what is going on in the world, what does this word make you think about? Describe in detail.
2. When you think about this word, how could it impact you and the relationships in your life? Describe in detail.
3. When you think about this word, what is stopping you from growing in this area of your life? Describe in detail.

Word 21: FRIENDSHIP

Definition

The relationship between friends; a friendly feeling or attitude; a kindness or help given to someone

Bible Verse

O for the days when I was in my prime. When God's intimate friendship blessed my house. ~ Job 29:4 NIV

Food for Thought

One of the most beautiful qualities of true friendship is to understand and be understood. ~ Lucius Seneca

Contemplation

Friendship is a strong bond. It is a connection like two links of a chain. Friendship is the capacity to truly understand someone else while at the same time be understood. Friendship is a two-way street. If we leave it just to ourselves to grow our own capacity, we're going to be limited in how big of a game we can play. We will also limit our ability to positively impact the world.

True friendship is the ability, not only to increase your capacity, but also to increase someone else's capacity. When you're connected in friendship with somebody else, your capacity has the opportunity to double, triple, or it even quadruple. Why? With the right intentions, friendship has the power to create a compounding effect of goodness in the world.

The magnificent design of the human race is that you are not limited by your own capacity to grow. Friendships last through good times, and they also last through bad times. Somebody whom I have a strong friendship with is a guy by the name of Kelly Ritchie who lives in Australia. He explained to me one time that in order to have a "We", there has to be a "You", and there has to be a "Me". It takes two people to create a "We". It takes two people to be involved in a friendship. That is a great design because we all know that life has ups and life has downs. When you have friendship with somebody else, it may work out that your ups and downs will occur at the same moment in time. However, very often, you may be up when your friend is down or vice versa. It's in these opposite up and down moments in life, that our friendships become strongly intertwined. The ups and downs become intertwined with somebody else, so over time, the bond of that friendship will be stronger as a result.

Your capacity will be increasing as a result. Your capacity for telling each other the truth ought to be growing. Your capacity for hearing and understanding will increase. Your capacity to learn and teach others will be increasing. Your capacity to have compassion and love others will be increasing. These qualities will determine the strength of your friendship, and it will determine the size of your capacity to grow.

∞

Empower Thought

Remember, you're not limited by your own capacity. If you really understand the truth of this word, friendship, you'll recognize that being connected with somebody else automatically increases your capacity because now you're dealing with more than one person's capacity. If a true friendship is there, you'll probably have very similar intentions for wanting to help and impact humanity in the world. Be grateful for all the friendships you have. The friendships that have allowed you to become the person that you are today, and the person that you're going to become tomorrow. I hope that you take the time to be grateful for this word, friendship.

Questions to Ponder

1. When you think of what is going on in the world, what does this word make you think about? Describe in detail.
2. When you think about this word, how could it impact you and the relationships in your life? Describe in detail.
3. When you think about this word, what is stopping you from growing in this area of your life? Describe in detail.

Word 22: GOODNESS

Definition

The quality or state of being; the nutritious, flavorful, or beneficial part of something

Bible Verse

But the fruit of the Spirit is love, joy, peace, patience, kindness, goodness, and faithfulness. ~ Galatians 5:22 NIV

Food for Thought

The fragrance of a flower spreads only in the direction of the wind, however, the goodness of a person spreads in all directions. ~ Chanakya

Contemplation

The goodness inside of you as a human has the capacity to spread in all directions, impacting everybody around you. The word goodness means to be nutritious, flavorful, and beneficial. Are you nutritious to other people? Are you flavorful to other people? Are you beneficial to other people? Are other people impacted positively from just being around you?

The word goodness has a strong analogy and association to fruit. Fruit is very healthy for you to eat on a daily basis. Fruit is beneficial and nutritious for you because of the vitamins that are contained within it. Most fruits grow on trees. So lets take an apple that is growing on a tree as an example. There is a phrase that says an apple a day keeps the doctor away. Apples have certain vitamins within them that are good and beneficial for you to eat. A tree produces them, but the tree must have roots that are deep. The same thing is true for you. If you want to have goodness inside of you, just like a tree, you will need to have some strong roots.

This root system has to pull water and nutrients out of the ground and bring it up though the base of the tree. The water and nutrients must then make their way through the core of the tree and out to the branches in order to produce an apple. Once the apple is ripe and hanging onto the outward branches, somebody can take it, eat it, and put inside of their body what was once inside of the tree and apple. In other words, the tree pulls nutrients out of the ground, internalizes them and uses them to produce the apple and shares it with the world.

The same process can become true for you as well. What is currently stopping you from building goodness inside of you? What kind of root system do you have? What kind of nutrients are you pulling up? What type of nutrients are you producing within you that may benefit other people?

∞

Empower Thought

Dr. Wayne Dyer often reminded people that you will not necessarily attract what you want life, rather, you will most likely attract what you are. You attract what you are! Wow! You are the nutrients that you're pulling up in life. You are your root system and you are your core beliefs. These are either producing bad fruit or they are producing good fruit. Take this word goodness, as an opportunity to look within and ask yourself, who is it that you are becoming? What's at your core? What kind of fruit do you bear for other people? Is it beneficial and nutritious for them?

Questions to Ponder

1. When you think of what is going on in the world, what does this word make you think about? Describe in detail.

2. When you think about this word, how could it impact you and the relationships in your life? Describe in detail.
3. When you think about this word, what is stopping you from growing in this area of your life? Describe in detail.

Word 23: GRACE

Definition

A way of moving that is smooth and attractive and that is not stiff

Bible Verse

It is by grace that you have been saved through faith, and this is not from yourselves it is a gift of God. ~ Ephesians 2:8 NIV

Food for Thought

Grace has been described as the outward expression of the inward harmony of the soul. ~ William Hazlitt

Contemplation

Do you desire to find a greater capacity for inward harmony? I believe the answer to this question for most is a resounding – YES! Life seems to throw most people out of sync with themselves. It seems that there is always somewhere to go, something to do and problems to solve with no time to accomplish it. I truly believe you deserve to pause and reflect on the inward harmony of your soul.

The definition of grace describes it as a way of moving through the world, a way of walking in this world that is smooth and attractive. Have you ever seen a great play on the soccer, baseball or football field? Have you ever watched a musician play an instrument while in a groove? Have you ever watched an ice-skater glide effortlessly across the ice? Have you ever watched a bird fly in the sky or the clouds move across the sky? Have you ever watched the wind blow the trees on a calm summer night? If so, you have witnessed grace in action. When we experience these moments in time, we see that they seem to occur with little or no effort. They appear to be doing exactly what they were designed to do. It makes you want more of it and something moves inside of you when you see a graceful player or moment.

Take a moment and reflect inwardly with the following questions because they help point to your purpose and passions in life.

- What is it that you do in this world that you believe is graceful for you?
- What do you do that seems effortless & smooth?
- What is something you love to do that is unique to you?
- What moves you internally that allows you to feel that you're in harmony with your soul?

I believe that life leaves little clues for us to find and unpack along our journey. Sometimes in life you are up and sometimes you are down. At other times you may feel really bad and un-ambitious, while at other times you feel completely inspired and motivated. Self-awareness is an important quality to growing your capacity for recognizing grace in your life. Your capacity for grace to grow internally begins the moment you acknowledge and honor your talents. Listen for the feedback. Listen for people to give you clues when they say, "...you're really good at that or have you ever thought about doing x, y or z with your life"? These are precious moments of grace that if you were to grab them and get passionate about them, you would move inwardly, in harmony with your soul. The more that you do that, the more you will become the person that you are pre-destined to become.

∞

Empower Thought

When it comes to living life more gracefully, most people live their lives backwards. They say things like, "Once I have all the things that I want, then I'll do all the things I need to do to become the person that I want to become." However, it is just the opposite in life with our word grace. If you want to move in a smooth and attractive way that is in harmony with your soul, then life requires you to become that person first.

By working on your inward harmony of your soul, you will ultimately move into doing those things that you should be doing. Soon, you will have the things you are seeking in life and it will appear to others that it is effortless to you. That's the challenge with this word grace, how to find something that is smooth, that is attractive, that is in harmony with your soul. You'll find that there are real deep truths inside of the word grace, and I hope you take the time to take a look at it.

Questions to Ponder

1. When you think of what is going on in the world, what does this word make you think about? Describe in detail.
2. When you think about this word, how could it impact you and the relationships in your life? Describe in detail.
3. When you think about this word, what is stopping you from growing in this area of your life? Describe in detail.

Word 24: GROWTH

Definition

A stage in the process of growing; progressive development

Bible Verse

A farmer went out to sow his seeds and as he was scattering seed some fell along the path and the birds came down and ate it up. Some fell on rocky places where it did not have much soil and it sprang up quickly because the soil was shallow but when the sun came out the plants were scorched and they withered because they had no roots. Other seed fell along the thorns, which grew up and choked the plants. Still other seed fell on good soil where it produced a crop 100, 60, 30 times what was sown. Whoever has ears let them hear. ~ Matthew 13:3-10 NIV

Food for Thought

Growth is not for everybody. Some people just want to stay the same forever. ~ Anonymous

Contemplation

Growth is a process of progressive development. It is worth understanding that whenever you are in a process; it means that you're moving from one spot to another spot. In other words, a process means that there is a direction to the movement within the process. Anytime you see the word process it means that something is moving and there's a direction to it. You are growing out of one scenario into a new scenario.

The word growth has the power to increase your capacity to become aware of the direction of your life. Think about the following questions:

- What are you growing out of and what are you growing into?
- What is the direction is your growth taking you?
- Is that a direction that's going to benefit you?
- Is that a direction that's going to grow you?
- Is that a direction that's going to increase your capacity?
- Is that a direction that's going to allow you to fulfill your passions and your purpose for living?
- What are you growing out of?
- What are you growing into?
- What is the trajectory of your growth?
- Are you getting bigger or are you getting smaller?

Some people can be heading in the right direction but ultimately it is shrinking them in terms of who they're supposed to be. Growth is a process and that means that it has directionality to it. It means that you're growing out of something and growing into something else. Make sure it's the right direction for you and then make sure you have the right trajectory. This will ensure that you are moving up and building your capacity as you're growing.

Have you ever heard the phrase, "You're either growing or you're dying"? Most people will make the mistake that it has to be one or the other. It does not have to be an either/or scenario; it truly is a both/and scenario. It's actually both because in order to grow, in my experience, some things have to die in order to grow. For example, to grow your fitness level, you will have to kill off eating bad foods and at the same time, you will have to grow in your ability to eat good foods. If you want to grow your knowledge of a certain subject, you have to kill off bad habits that waste time and grow into the habit of reading, absorbing, thinking and learning.

∞

Empower Thought

Remember, anytime you're in a growth process it's not that you're either growing or you're dying, it's that you actually have to do both. In order to grow out of something and grow into something else, you have to kill off some bad desires and temptations in order to grow and realize your purpose and passion for your life. That's a big, big challenge but I want you to recognize that growth is a process. You're growing out of something and into something else. There is a direction to growth and that direction has a trajectory. It's an evolutionary process for you.

Questions to Ponder

1. When you think of what is going on in the world, what does this word make you think about? Describe in detail.
2. When you think about this word, how could it impact you and the relationships in your life? Describe in detail.
3. When you think about this word, what is stopping you from growing in this area of your life? Describe in detail.

Word 25: HAPPINESS

Definition

A state of being happy; a pleasurable or satisfying experience

Bible Verse

His master replied, "Well done, good and faithful servant. You have been faithful with a few things. I will put you in charge of many things. Come and share your master's happiness." ~ Matthew 25:21 NIV

Food for Thought

For every minute that you are angry, you lose 60 seconds of happiness.
~ Anonymous

Contemplation

We all recognize and have experienced this powerful emotion called happiness. Most look for ways to pursue it and get more of it. Is it possible to be happy all of the time? The reality of living life on earth is that you're not going to be happy all of the time. The way that we live in the world will begin to change when we can unpack this word happiness a little bit more and gain clarity on what happiness is and what it is not.

Going back to the dictionary definition, it says happiness is a state of being happy, or it's an experience. The important thing to remember is that happiness is a state or an experience. Pause for a moment, close your eyes and ask yourself the following:

- When was a time in your life that you were most happy?
- How long was it?

- Where were you?
- What else was going on?
- What was it that you were honoring about yourself when you were in a state of being happy?

I believe that the more often you can look back and shine a light on all the times that you were happy, you'll begin to realize you have an enormous capacity to experience happiness. By awakening your senses to the experience, you will actually be able to re-experience the emotion of happiness.

- When was it?
- Where was it?
- Who was around?
- What was it that you were doing?

With this word happiness, there is a big difference between attaching happiness to things versus people that make you happy. Ask yourself the following, "Is your happiness connected to a "What" or is it connected to a "Whom"?

Over the years, I have had a unique opportunity to be around a lot of very successful people in terms of fame and wealth. Most people assume that the more things you acquire equal the amount of happiness in your life. These things that you can acquire, I will call the "What's" of life. The "What's" could include a new house, a new car, an expensive vacation, a new phone, a new computer, a new job, or a new business. Most people will also choose a belief system that says they cannot be happy unless they have all of the "What's". This belief system is way off course. The radical reality of the word happiness isn't found in the "What's".

Let's take a look at how this type of scenario plays out in real life. Let's say that you have just purchased the latest phone because your happiness, you thought, was connected to you having this new phone. You couldn't wait to have this new phone and once you purchased it, that new phone made you happy for probably the first couple days. Pretty soon however, over time, it became just a phone you used just like the older one. Soon your happiness began to get smaller and smaller and smaller. Then another newer version of the phone came out. Soon you become dissatisfied with the phone you recently purchased and now you have to get another new phone to make you happy. So what once made you happy no longer is making you happy anymore.

This same scenario could be true for a car, for a house, for a boat, or anything that could fall into the category of a "What". This is why we have to be extremely careful trying to define and attach our happiness to the category of the "What's". I want challenge you to get out of the "What's" category and get into the "Who's" category. Who makes you most happy? Happiness can truly be found in a who, not in a what. Who has the greatest impact on your life? Who are you around, that when you're around them your happiness begins to increase?

∞

Empower Thought

It is a powerful moment to realize happiness is found inside of a "Whom" as opposed to a "What". I challenge you to look at your happiness and find the times that you were most happy. Become aware of the types of relationships you are growing and with whom. Doing this will increase your capacity for happiness and the way you live in the world will begin to change as a result.

Questions to Ponder

1. When you think of what is going on in the world, what does this word make you think about? Describe in detail.
2. When you think about this word, how could it impact you and the relationships in your life? Describe in detail.
3. When you think about this word, what is stopping you from growing in this area of your life? Describe in detail.

Word 26: HEALTH

Definition

The condition of being well or free from disease; being sound in body, mind and spirit

Bible Verse

For they are life to those who find them and health to one's whole body.
~ Proverbs 4:22 NIV

Food for Thought

Love yourself enough to live a healthy lifestyle. ~ Anonymous

Contemplation

You deserve to have and live a healthy life. The challenge is to love your self enough to want to live a healthy lifestyle. Most people, if given the choice between being healthy or unhealthy, would choose to be healthy. Yet so many people live an unhealthy lifestyle.

Let's break apart the word healthy into the three categories called body, mind, and spirit. Some people may find that they have the ability to live a healthy lifestyle in one of the categories versus the other two. If we want to change the way that we live in the world, we will need to increase our capacity to live a healthy lifestyle in all three categories simultaneously.

Let's start with a healthy body. There is really only two things you really need to do in order to have a healthy body, eat right and exercise. That's it. Two things. Eat right and exercise. You can go online and you'll find hundreds of thousands of methodologies on how to eat right and hundreds of thousands of methodologies on how to exercise, but it's really the only two things that you need to do. You just need to research and apply the methodology that works best for you. What is a working methodology for you to eat right and what is a working methodology for you to exercise? Once you find them, I challenge you to apply them every single day. Every single day, live a healthy lifestyle with your body. You're given just one body. Your body is unique and it is a living, breathing miracle. You need to feed it properly and you need to move it and exercise it daily.

The second category is a healthy mind. Like the body, our minds need to be exercised every single day. There are three primary ways to exercise the mind daily.

1. Reading something daily.
2. Think about what you are reading and the impact those things could have on your life daily.
3. Discussing with others what you are learning.

A healthy mind is reading, thinking, and discussing daily. I think that if you did those things every single day, your capacity is going to begin to increase and your ability to be impactful in the world will increase as well.

The third category is a healthy spirit. My experience points towards this one being the most powerful. You ought to start your day thinking about how to have a healthy spiritual lifestyle.

- Do you pray every day?
- Do you meditate every day?
- Are you finding ways to be grateful daily?

Prayer, meditation, and gratitude are capacity building exercises for your spirit. If you did those three things every day, you would find that the health of your spirit would increase. As a result, your drive to live a life on purpose will begin to increase. It's your spirit that's going to comfort you. It's your spirit that's going to give you purpose for getting up and going out into the world.

∞

Empower Thought

You owe it to yourself to have a strong body, a strong mind, and a strong spirit. Having a strong spirit will propel your desire for a strong body and mind. Combined together, these three elements will give you the capacity to impact people in the way that I believe you're designed to impact people. I challenge you to do that every single day. Think about your spirit, think about your mind, and think about your body. Love yourself enough to want to life a healthy lifestyle. Be disciplined at doing it every single day of every single week of every single month of every single year for the rest of your life, and the way that you live in the world will begin to change.

Questions to Ponder

1. When you think of what is going on in the world, what does this word make you think about? Describe in detail.
2. When you think about this word, how could it impact you and the relationships in your life? Describe in detail.
3. When you think about this word, what is stopping you from growing in this area of your life? Describe in detail.

Word 27: HEART

Definition

An organ in your chest that pumps blood through your veins and through your arteries; one's innermost character, feelings or inclinations

Bible Verse

Whatever you do, work at it with all your heart, as working for the Lord, not for human masters. ~ Colossians 3:23 NIV

Food for Thought

"It's impossible", said Pride. "It's risky", said Experience. "It's pointless", said Reason. "Give it a try", whispered your Heart. ~ Anonymous

Contemplation

While the dictionary definitions seem very different, a closer look reveals that they're actually merged together in a pretty important way. The first part of the definition says that heart is an organ that pumps blood through your veins and through your arteries. I think that most of us can recognize that. Thinking more deeply about the word heart, we can also recognize heart as our innermost character. Let's take each one separately and then put them together.

First, think about the word heart as an organ. The heart pumps blood through your body, it's going through your veins and through your arteries. While alive, your heart is constantly pumping and pumping and pumping and pumping. Its job is to move your blood all the way through your body, all the way down to your extremities. Your heart is extremely powerful. Your blood contains blood cells that carry nutrients within them, ultimately depositing these nutrients to different parts of your body all day long, so that the cells in these different parts of your body can do what they do. They can grow your fingernails, grow your skin, grow your hair, it allows your senses to work and everything else that goes on within your body. It's an important process in your body. The moment your heart stops pumping, there would be no more blood and no more oxygen getting to your body, then ultimately, your body would decay.

The same thing is true for your life. When you think about the word heart as your innermost character, look to see the purity of your heart. Look to recognize your reason for being alive and what it is that you're ultimately pursuing. Your innermost character acts like a beating heart. Your character is what beats every single day that carries itself into all of your conversations, into all of your intentions, into all of your thoughts, into all of your feelings, into all of your emotions, into all of your interactions and into everything that you do business-wise, family-wise, etc. Your innermost character is like this beating heart that is constantly pumping, pumping, and pumping. This gives us a very good opportunity to pause and to reflect.

- What is the beating heart of your character?
- What are your innermost desires and passions?
- If we could cut you open and look at the heart of your character, what is it that you want to be true about you?
- What is it that you want to pump out and how far can it pump itself out?
- What are the nutrients of your hearts character that you pump into other people?
- What do you want your hearts character to pump into the world?

∞

Empower Thought

It is an empowering point of reference to think about how our hearts character beats in a rhythm, much like the heart as an organ. There is an in, and there is an out. There's an in and there's an out to our character. When we take the time to look at the two definitions coming together, we see that they also share the same obstacle to performance.

The heart has to pump much harder when there's a blockage somewhere in a vein or artery. The same thing is true for you and your character, often times; we will experience blockages either on the inside or the outside of our life. When this happens, we have to do that much more work on our character in order to pump out our innermost character into the world. We have to basically diagnose our own pumping mechanism called our character and see where there are blockages in our system. Are there blockages on things that are coming into our thoughts and into our belief systems? Or, are the blockages occurring on the way out? Your innermost character does have a rhythm and timing to it. There is an in and there is an out to it. My hope for you is that you pause and reflect on this word, heart. Become aware of your innermost character and what are you pumping in and what are you pumping out?

Questions to Ponder

1. When you think of what is going on in the world, what does this word make you think about? Describe in detail.
2. When you think about this word, how could it impact you and the relationships in your life? Describe in detail.
3. When you think about this word, what is stopping you from growing in this area of your life? Describe in detail.

Word 28: HEAVEN

Definition

The place where God lives and where good people go after they die
according to some religions

Bible Verse

In the beginning, God created the heavens and the earth.
~ Genesis 1:1 NIV

Food for Thought

Joy is the serious business of heaven. ~ CS Lewis

Contemplation

Regardless of where you live in the world or what your belief
system is, most people over the course of human history; think of heaven
as a positive place. I've never met anybody in all of my global travels, talk
about this word heaven in a negative way. They don't picture it as evil.
They don't picture it as someplace that's bad. They don't picture it as
someplace that they don't want to belong to. Most people would love the
opportunity to live the rest of their life in a state or place called heaven.
People use words like bright, clean, wondrous, peaceful, joyous, magical,
and mysterious to describe heaven. Most people say, "I hope that I get
there and I hope that I can be in everlasting communion with God." This
word heaven is worth serious contemplation.

The word or thought of heaven has significantly shaped the way
that I see things in the world. It has shaped the way that I hear things in the
world. It has most definitely shaped the way that I move, interact, and

build relationships in this world. Heaven deserves our researching it, thinking about it, reading about it, praying about it, meditating about it, discussing it, and debating it with others. Heaven deserves a daily conversation.

There are a lot of places to research this word heaven. There are so many religions and spiritual teachers on the topic of heaven. You owe it to your spirit to listen and read all the information you can about heaven and seek out its truth. I can guarantee you; the truth will set you free when you recognize the truth. You will recognize the truth when you hear it. You may just realize that as you are seeking out the truth of the word heaven, heaven has actually been seeking you out! That is power!

The truth of what heaven is will come seeking you out the more you begin to open up your mind, open up your eyes, and open up your heart to the idea of heaven. It will open up the capacity for you to begin a conversation that builds an eternal foundation for you.

You don't want to be ignorant to the truth of heaven. If you aspire to get to a magical place like heaven, then you deserve not to be ignorant. This means you're going to have to put some work in to read and study and listen and contemplate. You will begin to understand what you were truly designed for, and you were designed to recognize truth.

Pause, reflect and look at how big the universe is. Regardless of how you think it may have come into existence, you can't deny the fact that the universe is majestic. The universe is extremely massive and constantly expanding. There are hundreds of billions of galaxies. There are hundreds of billions of stars in each galaxy. There's also a very unique place called Earth that was created within this universe that happens to have the exact right conditions for human life. You just have to contemplate that – daily! On earth, we have the unique opportunity to see and walk on a beach, watch endless waves crash on a shore, see the sun rise and see the sun set, you can see a mountaintop or climb to the top of it, you see a great painting, you see a loved one, you can play or listen to great music, you can eat a piece of chocolate cake, or take a lick of an ice cream cone. If you look hard enough, you will see the gears of heaven at work in everything you experience.

∞

Empower Thought

Earth is just a glimpse into heaven. It is the curtain being pulled back just a little bit of what I believe heaven is going to be like. Just look at the universe and you will see a tiny little glimpse of what heaven can ultimately be like for you. It's worth the conversation. It's worth the journey. It's worth the contemplation. It's worth the debate. You should think about heaven every single day for the rest of your life because the way that you live in the world will significantly change. The truth will find you, it will set you forever free, and you'll be so grateful that it did.

Questions to Ponder

1. When you think of what is going on in the world, what does this word make you think about? Describe in detail.
2. When you think about this word, how could it impact you and the relationships in your life? Describe in detail.
3. When you think about this word, what is stopping you from growing in this area of your life? Describe in detail.

Word 29: HOPE

Definition

To want something to happen; to cherish a desire with anticipation

Bible Verse

For I know the plans that I have for you, declares the Lord. Plans to prosper you and not to harm you. Plans to give you hope and a future.
~ Jeremiah 29:11 NIV

Food for Thought

Hope sees the invisible and feels the intangible. ~ Anonymous

Contemplation

All of us can recognize that there are things invisible and intangible to us, however, hope sees the invisible. Hope allows you to look for something you desire in the future with anticipation. The future you're hoping for is at some moment in the distance that's not quite here yet; it's somewhere out there. You're hopeful with anticipation that what you think you're seeing out there is going to ultimately come through and you're going to be able to see it, touch it and experience it.

So many people lose hope. So many people give up on life because their hopes and dreams seem invisible, intangible and impossible. I challenge you today to pause and reflect on this word hope. Allow hope to boil over inside of you, allow hope to simmer deep inside of your spirit and allow hope to provide you with a glimpse into your future. There is so much radical reality inside of the word hope. Hope is a word of action. Hope is a word of great behavior and a word that has the power for you to

84

visualize your future. Maybe you can't touch it and maybe it seems impossible, but hope is going to build capacity inside of you that will change the way that you live in the world.

It is worth contemplating the following questions regarding hope.

- What are you most hopeful for?
- What you hope for; is it going to happen in a day?
- Is it going to happen in a week?
- Is it going to happen in a month?
- Is it going to happen in a year or it's going to happen over your lifetime?
- How far out does this hope travel for you?

Let me provide you an analogy to help us understand hope. I am confident that you have seen a sailboat. All sailboats have a sail and a sailboat is able to move towards a destination regardless of the direction of the winds that are blowing. Let's say that you set out on a sailboat and you had a hopeful desire to sail to a beautiful island with pristine beaches where the sun was always shining. When we set sail, we are unable to see the island with our eyes. We can't see that it is there, but we set sail anyways and wait in hopeful anticipation that we are able to navigate our way to it. So it is in life, as you head out to achieve a desired goal, you have to head out with this hopeful ambition that you're going to get there. Along the way, people get discouraged because the winds begin to blow. They blow from the right and all of a sudden the winds shift and start to blow from the left. This doesn't mean that you can't get to where you need to get. It just means that you need to change the angle of the sail so it can catch the shifting conditions that the world is providing to you at that moment in time. You can still get to your hopeful destination, if you do not bail out.

The question then becomes:

- How are you setting the sails of your life?
- What is the intention behind your sails?
- Where do you hope to go?
- What do you hope for today?
- What do you hope for this week? Month? Year?
- What do you hope for the next 3, 5, 10, 15 years? Your entire life?

∞

Empower Thought

What do you hope for during your lifetime? When your life comes to an end, what do you hope with anticipation happens afterwards? This is a powerful question to ask around this word hope. It's worth contemplating because if you look beyond the horizon of your lifetime into eternity, it may have the power to change the way that you arrange the sails of your life. Ultimately, the way that you live in the world will begin to change.

Questions to Ponder

1. When you think of what is going on in the world, what does this word make you think about? Describe in detail.
2. When you think about this word, how could it impact you and the relationships in your life? Describe in detail.
3. When you think about this word, what is stopping you from growing in this area of your life? Describe in detail.

Word 30: HUMILITY

Definition

Quality or state of not thinking that you are better than other people; the act or posture of lowering oneself in relation to others

Bible Verse

Do nothing out of selfish ambition or vain conceit. Rather, in humility, value others above yourselves, not looking to your own interests, but each of you to the interests of others. ~ Philippians 2:3-4 NIV

Food for Thought

Humility is not thinking less of yourself, but thinking of yourself less. ~ CS Lewis

Contemplation

For those that want to be leaders, how do you lead other people with humility? How can you be a leader when the definition of humility says, "the posture of lowering oneself in relation to others"? This has been a stumbling block for many leaders and especially for people that aspire to be leaders. Most leaders push hard, demand respect, they drive a big mission and vision. They want people to follow them. They believe that they need to be hard charging, high ego, stellar inspiration and high-octane motivation. The challenge is how to work through people in a way with humility where you can still have the strength and power of a leader, but do it in a way that is not for self-interests, but rather for the interest of others.

- When was the last time you lowered yourself in service to somebody else?
- When was the last time you were a catalyst for others, not because you wanted to be seen as a leader, but because you aspired to see other people grow?

Humility is the ability to value others above yourself. It has become a challenge for most of us because of our belief systems that we have developed over our lifetime. We have adopted belief systems that reward the self-motivated. We look to self-help books, self-improvement seminars and self-development programs. While these can play a role, the problem is they are all focused on "self". If left un-checked, these tools could actually create a shield or a barrier to your ability to move through the world with humility.

These "self" belief systems can begin building in most youth sports teams. Are you a starter in that sport, or are you somebody that comes in off the bench? If you are a starter, are you the captain of the team? This then morphs into who are the group of friends that you hang out with? Are you part of the "in crowd" or are you just part of a different crowd? Are you the leader of the crowd or are you part of no crowd at all? Then you go off to college and you're asked to choose a major. This narrows your focus from others again to "self". You pursue a focus that may lead you to a good career. Why? Because most are interested in their self and what will be in it for them at the end. People will ask you, "Who do you want to become" and "What are your priorities in life"? Then ultimately when you graduate with a degree in a certain field of study, you will get a job and usually start at the bottom. It will not be long and all your self-motivations will start to creep in. You may begin to say, "I want to make my mark in the world" or "I want to move up the ranks through this corporate ladder," or, "I want to go and pursue and start my own business." Those conversations with yourself are predominantly driven by self-interests. If we're not careful, these self-interests can creep in, build, and develop our belief systems that stay there through our entire lives.

The challenge with this word humility is to find a way to work hard with all of your heart, while at the same time being in the service to others. Would you trust that you could attain success while putting yourself lower in service to other people? Not because you are weaker than somebody else, but because you're stronger than somebody else. Everybody needs somebody to guide them along the paths of life. Everybody needs somebody to lead them, and everybody deserves to have a leader that is not self-interested and self-motivated, but rather, other people focused.

∞

Empower Thought

Humility can begin by remembering that you did not make you. You were designed and predestined to accomplish great things with your life. The golden rule of love others as you want to be loved is a solid leadership principle that can make you a stronger leader, not a weaker one. This word humility has power within it, pause and reflect on your understanding and application of this word, it can change the way you live in the world.

Questions to Ponder

1. When you think of what is going on in the world, what does this word make you think about? Describe in detail.
2. When you think about this word, how could it impact you and the relationships in your life? Describe in detail.
3. When you think about this word, what is stopping you from growing in this area of your life? Describe in detail.

Word 31: INSPIRATION

Definition

A force or influence that inspires someone to want to do something, or that gives someone an idea about what to do or create

Bible Verse

All of scripture is God breathed and useful for teaching, rebuking, correcting, and training in righteousness. ~ 2 Timothy 3:16 NIV

Food for Thought

I haven't failed; I've just found 10,000 ways that do not work.
~ Thomas Edison

Contemplation

What inspires you? What are you most inspired about in your life currently? Before you answer too quickly, let's pause and reflect on the definition of the word inspiration to find some truth. The definition says that inspiration is a force or influence that inspires someone to want to do something, or that gives someone an idea about what to do or create. Two key words emerge out of the definition, force and influence. Where does this force come from and what is it trying to influence in your life? Are you even aware that these 2 dynamics are at play in your life?

It is also worth noting that there is a world of difference between the word inspiration and the word motivation. Many people can get the two confused or they make the mistake that they are synonyms. They are not. One is "a priori" or more important than the other one. Inspiration is way more powerful than motivation. If you have inspiration you will become motivated to move towards an inspired idea. However, you cannot create enough motivation to give birth to inspiration. Therefore, if inspiration is way more powerful than motivation, where does the force and influence of inspiration come from and why is it so different from motivation?

This is the major difference; motivation is you trying to grab hold of an idea. Inspiration, on the other hand, is an idea that grabs a hold of you. Inspiration is an idea that grabs a hold of you and influences you to move towards a desired outcome. So, where does the force of inspiration come from? It comes from being in spirit. Inspiration comes from being in spirit. Since we are in a constant battle between our ego and our spirit, it is often difficult to truly appreciate inspiration. The ego will lean on motivation while the spirit will lean on inspiration. Do not let the ego fool you – stay in spirit!

The powerful truth of this word inspiration is that it's an idea that grabs a hold of you. It will create the motivation necessary for you to fulfill its mission. You can get "in-spirit" or "in-tune" with your spirit through prayer, meditation, thinking and contemplation. You truly owe it to yourself to spend a lot more time than you currently do being "in-spirit". Find a couple of times a day to sit with yourself "in-spirit" and allow inspiration to grab a hold of you. Recognize that you may be blocking it with your ego and you may be blocking it with motivation because you think you should be doing something besides sitting "in-spirit". Listen and pay attention to what is quietly stirring inside of you.

- What is the spark that's been lit inside of you?
- What is the flame of truth that's lying dormant inside of you?
- What if that flame of inspiration is in danger of being extinguished – by you?

Something else to consider with inspiration, is that you need to allow yourself enough time to recognize it and develop it. I believe that inspiration takes time. I believe that your life could be compared to a chunk of coal that is being put under a lot of pressure. If a chunk of coal is put under enough pressure, over a period of time with intense fire and heat, that chunk of coal has the opportunity to turn into a diamond. Coal has an opportunity to turn into a diamond. The same thing is true for you as you move through this word inspiration. Your life is like a chunk of coal that's being refined and pressurized and you can become a beautiful, shiny, crystal-clear diamond. The really cool thing about a chunk of coal turning into a diamond is that the process is irreversible. If you allow yourself the opportunity to get "in-spirit" and find your true inspiration that comes from within I believe that your life will change.

∞

Empower Thought

Remember, inspiration is an idea that grabs hold of you. Motivation is you trying to grab hold of an idea. Motivation is driven by ego. Inspiration is driven by spirit. And so I hope that you take the time to ponder that today. Let your spirit rise up, let your spirit influence you, let your spirit inspire you!

Questions to Ponder

1. When you think of what is going on in the world, what does this word make you think about? Describe in detail.
2. When you think about this word, how could it impact you and the relationships in your life? Describe in detail.
3. When you think about this word, what is stopping you from growing in this area of your life? Describe in detail.

Word 32: KNOWLEDGE

Definition

Information, understanding, or skills that you get from experience or education

Bible Verse

For this reason, make every effort to add to your faith, goodness, and to goodness, knowledge. ~ 2 Peter 1:5 NIV

Food for Thought

As knowledge increases, wonder deepens. ~ Charles Morgan

Contemplation

As knowledge increases it has the opportunity to deepen your wonder. Once knowledge starts to peel itself open, it is like a whole new frontier reveals itself. Knowledge is a magical resource in the world, the more you use it, the more it grows. Knowledge will never be depleted.

If we go back to the definition for a moment, it says knowledge is information, understanding, or skills that you can get from experience or from education. The two key words within the definition of knowledge are in understanding how to get it - "experience" and "education". These are the two types of knowledge that can be acquired. One is educational knowledge, which can be acquired through reading books, taking a course, going to seminars, reading online, watching a video, or listening to a podcast. This type of knowledge increases your ability to "know about" something. To "know about" is a great starting point. However, there is a great shift that can occur in your capacity when you move from "knowing about" something, and you actually applying it in your life. During that moment of application, you move into the second type of knowledge, which is the "experience of it".

As you develop "experience" knowledge, you begin to build a knowledge base that your knowingness comes from within as opposed to outside sources. This is the type of knowledge that deepens your sense of wonder. "Experience" knowledge can light the flames of inspiration and intention for your life. It will also set the sails for the direction that you want to go in life.

There are so many things out there to learn about. There are so many opportunities to acquire knowledge, but where you become most effective, to impact the most amount of people, is to find a knowledge area of life that you can become most passionate about. An area of knowledge that really lights you up, that really creates a sense of wonder and awe for your spirit.

- What is a subject that you want to acquire "educational" knowledge of?
- What is a subject that you want to acquire "experiential" knowledge of?
- Do you want to know about the universe?
- Do you want to know about spiritual matters?
- Do you want to know about the design of humans?
- Do you want to know about money?
- Do you want to know about business?
- Do you want to know about relationships?
- Do you want to know about global affairs?

∞

Empower Thought

Knowledge is an infinite resource, meaning it's not like oil, it's not like gas, where there's only a finite, limited quantity of it in the world. Knowledge is infinite, the more that you use it, the more that it grows. The more you experience it, the more you can share it. That's such an awesome quality of the nature of knowledge. When you increase your educational and experiential knowledge, you become more effective, more efficient, and you become a greater catalyst for other people to want to grow. You begin to add value to other people. You move from learning to leading, from leading to influencing, and from influencing to empowering others.

Questions to Ponder

1. When you think of what is going on in the world, what does this word make you think about? Describe in detail.
2. When you think about this word, how could it impact you and the relationships in your life? Describe in detail.
3. When you think about this word, what is stopping you from growing in this area of your life? Describe in detail.

Word 33: LIFE

Definition

The ability to grow or change

Bible Verse

The Lord God formed a man form the dust of the ground and breathed into
his nostrils the breath of life, and the man became a living being.
~ Genesis 2:7 NIV

Food for Thought

When I was born, I was so surprised that I did not speak for the first year
and a half. ~ Anonymous

Contemplation

All would agree that life is extremely important, vital, and precious.
We all want to experience the most out of life. We dream of and pursue
different experiences during our lifetime. We also want our life to matter.
When I think about life, I think about life as an experience. I often say, "Ride
the Wave of Life & PlayBig!!" Life is the ability to grow, life is the ability to
change, and life is an experience unlike any other.

To better understand the word life, I would like to share with you
an acronym of the word life, or L.I.F.E. We will look at the "L," the "I," the
"F," and the "E" that make up the word life.

- L: Stands for Learning
- I: Stands for Investing
- F: Stands for Facilitating
- E: Stands for Expanding

The "L" in the word life stands for learning. Life allows us the opportunity to learn. There are all kinds of things to learn about in this world. There are all kinds of books to read, places to go, courses to take and people to communicate with. However, when thinking about learning, I challenge you to learn about the most important questions in life:

- Why were you born?
- What is your purpose?
- What is your calling?
- Where do you learn about these areas?
- Who do you learn from?
- How often do you make learning a priority?
- Are you a lifelong learner?

The second letter is "I", which stands for investing. I am not talking about investing money into a stock market or into a business. The letter "I" in life means to "invest" into relationships.

- What is the most predominant relationship you currently have that is guiding your life?
- Who do you invest your time and energy into?
- What type of return is your life getting from these investments in or with others?
- Who should you invest more in?

The third letter is "F", which stands for facilitate. If we're learning, and we're investing in relationships, then it becomes important to pay attention to the types of communications we are facilitating. Facilitating allows you to become a catalyst for others to ponder their own life. You can facilitate what you are learning, both positive and negative. This is a powerful life learning design of humans, to facilitate life's big issues through the generations. Hopefully, this will allow the future generations to know and understand truth, as well as, have an easier path in life.

Finally, we get to "E", which stands for expand. If you become a lifelong learner, if you're learning how to invest your energy and time wisely, and if you're facilitating conversations about what you're learning, you can't help but to expand yourself. You can't help but to expand your capacity. Ultimately, you're going to expand the capacity for others to grow and change themselves. Changing not only the way that you live in the world, but others – true empowerment!

∞

Empower Thought

If you look at the word life as an acronym, L.I.F.E., it will allow for you to have a much richer life experience. Your life will increase in its capacity to grow and change. Pause and reflect on the word life – and always remember to "Ride the Wave of Life & PlayBig!!"

Questions to Ponder

1. When you think of what is going on in the world, what does this word make you think about? Describe in detail.
2. When you think about this word, how could it impact you and the relationships in your life? Describe in detail.
3. When you think about this word, what is stopping you from growing in this area of your life? Describe in detail.

Word 34: LOVE

Definition

A feeling of strong and constant affection for a person

Bible Verse

Dear friends, let us love one another, for love comes from God. Everyone who loves has been born of God and knows God. ~ 1 John 4:7 NIV

Food for Thought

Someone who really loves you sees what a mess you can be, how moody you can get, how hard you are to handle, but still wants you in their life.
~ Anonymous

Contemplation

We all know that we can be mean, messy, moody and hard to handle at times, yet we have people in our lives that still love us. That's such a great feeling to have. The definition of our word love describes two of its primary qualities, "strong" and "constant". When we experience love, we want it to be strong and we want it to be constant. The question then becomes where does its strength come from and how does it stay constant?

So where does love's strength come from? In order to understand the strength of love, it may be beneficial to look at the opposite of love, which is fear. Where there is strength of love, there is no fear. Love and fear cannot co-exist at the same moment in time within us. The problem is most people live more of their life in fear than they do in love. Why? The reason is so many of us are in constant worry and anxiety about our life, our health, our finances, our family, our friends, our career, etc. This means that the amount of love that they're experiencing is greatly diminished. Fear sets up camp within our emotions, thoughts and our belief systems. When this occurs, it becomes a vicious circle that becomes difficult to break.

- What are you fearful of?
- What are you anxious about?
- When was the last time you felt loved?
- When was the last time you used love to drive out fear?
- Do you have more fearful thoughts or loving thoughts? Why?

If we are not careful, as our love within loses power, it becomes less constant in our lives. When we lose the strength of love, we don't have the constant love that's there because we're weakened by this idea of fear. However, when you start to experience love, you will become aware of its strength. As the strength of love begins to build back up and as fear begins to diminish, you will recognize that love is a constant. You will become aware of the strength and constant affection that shows through your mind, through your body, through your soul, and through your heart. Once it starts pouring through, fear begins to dissipate. Fear begins to go away, and you increase your capacity to change and influence the way that you live in the world.

∞

Empower Thought

One of the things that I know can begin to build love up inside of you is remembering who you are, where you come from, and why you're here. In particular, if you're to look at a DNA strand that's inside of every single cell of your body, it will allow you to remember that you are so unique, that you were born in an unbelievable way, that there's no human that's ever walked the face of the earth that has your DNA strand exactly. There's no human currently living that has the exact same DNA that you have right now. When you look at that, it's a reminder to you that you are a living, breathing miracle. You have been fearfully and wonderfully made. I honestly believe that about you. You need to fall back in love with this idea that you are a living, breathing-miracle. There is a reason that you're alive and there's a purpose for your life. When you tap into that, love starts to come pouring through your mind, body, and spirit. Love is strong and love is constant.

Questions to Ponder

1. When you think of what is going on in the world, what does this word make you think about? Describe in detail.
2. When you think about this word, how could it impact you and the relationships in your life? Describe in detail.
3. When you think about this word, what is stopping you from growing in this area of your life? Describe in detail.

Word 35: MONEY

Definition

A way to pay for goods and services; something generally accepted as a medium of exchange or a measure of value

Bible Verse

No one can serve two masters. Either you will hate the one or love the other, or you'll be devoted to the one and despise the other. You cannot serve both God and money. ~ Matthew 6:24 NIV

Food for Thought

Money will not create success, but the freedom to make it will.
~ Nelson Mandela

Contemplation

Money does not create success. I have been blessed to travel and interact with people from all the world and anytime somebody important starts speaking about the word "money", people begin to lean in, their eyes get big and their ears open up wide. The reason is because everybody wants to know how to make money, how to make big money, and how to do it while they sleep.

Surprise! I'm not going to talk about how to make money or how to make big money because that is not my calling in life. However, I do want to share with you my perspective of the word "money" so that you may have an opportunity to not be a slave to money. It is sad to see how many people have become slaves to money. You can go anywhere in the world and watch how much time and energy is devoted during someone's life, all in an effort to just make money. Very few people have taken the time to pause and reflect on the truth of what money actually is.

If we go back to the dictionary definition, it says money is "a medium of exchange". A couple of important questions to ponder:

- What do you exchange for money?
- Is it worth it? Are you worth it?
- What do you exchange your money for?
- Is it worth it?
- Are you a slave to money?

People will spend a lifetime trying to get money because they want to exchange it for so many other things. Our society is great at creating a perceived value of money and things. However, if you can really understand what money is you'll become less of a slave to it.

Money is really nothing more than a storage device. For example, I live in the United States, and so the United States government and the banking system create the value of what one US dollar is equal to. There is not much that you or I can do to change what the value of one US dollar is worth. We just need to know that one US dollar is worth something. Therefore, one US dollar has storage of value that determines what we can exchange for one US dollar. If I take that one US dollar and I go into another country, that other country is going to tell me what it's worth. There are rules to the global game of money. We are not going to change that, so we need to become aware that money is a storage device or a measure of value.

Money has become such an important tool within the world that it has a gravitational pull on people's lives. Unfortunately for most, it is actually pulling them away from and shrinking their capacity, shrinking their dreams, shrinking their hopes and shrinking their passions. It is often sad to see all the wasted energy just to make money. Most will become aware too late in life and never have the energy to go and pursue their dreams.

- Are you more interested in economic profit or are you more interested in human profit?
- Do you care more about money or do care more about people?

- Do you spend more time thinking about money wealth or spiritual wealth?
- How long will your money wealth last you?
- How long will your spirit wealth last you?

I believe all of us have the ability to add value to another human.

Maybe you're more designed for human profit, but your desire for economic profit is driving you in a direction that you don't want to go. Years ago I read a book by R. Buckminster Fuller called "Critical Path" and he asked the questions, "Are you willing to do things that make sense and trust that you'll make money?" Most people live life just the opposite, they do things to make money and trust that what they do to make money will make sense. I challenge you to do things that make sense and trust that you'll end up making money. I believe if you lived life this way, your value to others would increase and others would exchange resources to have you around.

∞

Empower Thought

Be careful with the direction you run for money because whatever direction you go, wherever you put your energy, your heart is going to follow that direction. I am sure that you don't want your heart running the way that most of the world is, which is to economic profit and money profit. Challenge yourself to look at the truth of the word "money" and shift your intention towards human profit, and trust that if you do things that make sense you would ultimately end up making money, and money is nothing more than a storage of value that is determined by somebody else.

Questions to Ponder

1. When you think of what is going on in the world, what does this word make you think about? Describe in detail.
2. When you think about this word, how could it impact you and the relationships in your life? Describe in detail.
3. When you think about this word, what is stopping you from growing in this area of your life? Describe in detail.

Word 36: PATIENCE

Definition

Able to remain calm and not become annoyed when waiting for a long period of time, or when dealing with problems or difficult people

Bible Verse

For in this hope we were saved, but hope that is seen is no hope at all. Who hopes for what they already have? But if we hope for what we do not yet have then we wait for it patiently. ~ Romans 8:24-25 NIV

Food for Thought

Patience is not only the ability to wait, but how we act while we wait. ~ Anonymous

Contemplation

Do you have the capacity to remain calm and not become annoyed when waiting on something? If you are like me, it seems that other people make it so easy to become annoyed by the crazy things they do or say. So many are more concerned with attaining a goal than they are with the person they are becoming. So many people just want to check things off their to-do list so they can say they've accomplished something.

- Are you more focused on to-do lists or must-do lists?
- Do you look for short cuts in life?
- Do you want the quick fix?
- Or do you want the right fix?
- On a scale of 1-10, how patient are you?
- If I were to ask 3 of your closest friends, would they describe you as a patient person?

Patience is a tremendous ability. A wise person once said that if you had the ability to have patience while you were waiting for a desired goal, you would begin to build another quality inside of you called perseverance. Then if you gave perseverance a chance to build inside of you, it would ultimately begin to shape your character. All of us want to grow our character, however, few of us realize that it starts with learning how to cultivate and grow this powerful word called patience. Everything in life has a gestation period. Some living things have a longer gestation period while others have a shorter gestation period. If that gestation period is altered, the finished product will be altered as well. Nature knows what it is doing; so let it do its work. The conditions that nature uses during the gestation period are called prevailing conditions.

Patience is a prevailing condition for real growth. Let me give you an example of how this works. You know what a flower is and you have no doubt witnessed a flower grow from nothing more than just a seed. What's important to recognize about a flower is that the sun does not cause the flower to grow, the rain does not cause a flower to grow, the fertilizer does not cause a flower to grow and dirt that the flower is planted in does not cause the flower to grow. However, when all of these conditions are present at the right time, in the right amount, then and only then, will the flower become what the flower was already predestined to become anyways. Patience is key to allowing the prevailing conditions to do their work!

∞

Empower Thought

The same thing is true for you. If you can pay attention to the prevailing conditions, the sunshine, the rain, the fertilizer, and the dirt, and in this case in your life that could be inspiration, motivation, patience, perseverance, character building. Whatever it may be, when the right conditions are appropriate and when the prevailing conditions are there, you too can become what you are already predestined to become anyways. Patience is a powerful word that gives us the opportunity to look and see, hear, and feel what these conditions are that are going to allow us to grow into and become what we were already predestined to become.

Questions to Ponder

1. When you think of what is going on in the world, what does this word make you think about? Describe in detail.
2. When you think about this word, how could it impact you and the relationships in your life? Describe in detail.
3. When you think about this word, what is stopping you from growing in this area of your life? Describe in detail.

Word 37: PEACE

Definition

A state in which there is no war and no fighting; harmony in personal relationships

Bible Verse

I have told you these things so that, in me, you may have peace. In this world you will have trouble, but take heart. I have overcome the world.
~ John 16:33 NIV

Food for Thought

Peace cannot be kept by force. It can only be achieved by understanding.
~ Albert Einstein

Contemplation

What is your current level of understanding about the word peace? The second part of the definition of the word peace says that it is harmony in personal relationships. Are you at peace with you? Are you at peace with others in your life? Why or Why not? These are difficult questions for most of us to answer because we would like to believe that we are at peace with ourselves. If we truly want to change the way that we live in the world, then we need to be honest with ourselves.

You may answer no I'm not at peace with the way that I interact in the world. You may say to yourself that there are things that I wish I hadn't said or there are behaviors I wish I could get rid of.

• When was the last time you felt at peace?

- Internally, do you feel more at peace or more at war with yourself?
- When you have peace how long does it last?
- Does it last a second, a minute, five minutes, or ten minutes? Longer?
- What is the longest length of time that you have experienced peace?
- How could you grow more peace if you were able to put awareness on it?
- What is a place or the environment that you're in that makes you feel most at peace?
- When you're feeling peace, how big does it seem?

Peace within ourselves, when looked at properly, can have a dimension to it. When you're at peace, learn to become aware of the harmony you feel with yourself. Next, become aware that you can actually feel internal harmony while the external world is in chaos. How can we build the capacity for internal peace when everything around us is in chaos? Think of the process like a force of nature called a hurricane. A hurricane is strong and violent. During a hurricane all kinds of debris is being torn up, spread around, thrown and tossed about. However, there is always an eye of the hurricane or the "eye of the storm". The eye of the hurricane is extremely calm and extremely silent. The same thing is true for you. When you put an "eye" or an "awareness" in the middle of your storm, it creates the opportunity to remain calm and in harmony. When you get at that moment of peace, you know that there are a lot of troubles in the world, but they do not have to affect you personally. Learn to grow your capacity for experiencing peace.

∞

Empower Thought

There is an old proverb that comes from a book called "The Tao Te Ching". One of the proverbs says that if you come across raging muddy waters in your life, recognize that it is nothing more than dirt mixed with water that happens to be in motion. Raging muddy water is nothing more than recognizing the fact that it's dirt mixed with water that happens to be in motion. So that's the same thing that happens in our lives. Most of us are so focused on the raging muddy water, all the currents, all the directions that we could go in life that we forget that it's really just dirt and water that happens to be in motion. In our case the dirt and water are our ego and spirit battling each other inside of us. Become aware that peace comes from your spirit. Learn to quiet the ego, settle the ego down or let the dirt settle to the bottom and you will soon recognize the clean, clear nature of your spirit.

Questions to Ponder

1. When you think of what is going on in the world, what does this word make you think about? Describe in detail.
2. When you think about this word, how could it impact you and the relationships in your life? Describe in detail.
3. When you think about this word, what is stopping you from growing in this area of your life? Describe in detail.

Word 38: PERSEVERANCE

Definition

The quality that allows someone to continue trying to do something even though it is difficult; continued effort to do or achieve something despite difficulties, failure or opposition.

Bible Verse

Not only so, but we also glory in our sufferings because we know that suffering produces perseverance and perseverance produces character and character produces hope. ~ Romans 5:3-4 NIV

Food for Thought

If you cannot fly, then run, and if you cannot run, then walk. And if you cannot walk, then crawl, but whatever you do you have to keep moving forward. ~ MLK, Jr.

Contemplation

The word perseverance seems to require a challenging experience. Life will ensure challenging moments for all of us. Some people will experience more challenging moments than others throughout life. However, I believe that we all have the capacity to persevere. The question is, where does the capacity to persevere come from? It can come from your ability to move through difficult and challenging circumstances with a lesson learned. Challenges are meant to grow and mature us, however, most people will not pause and reflect long enough to get the lesson – so the challenges repeat themselves until we learn the lesson. Life is an experience, both good ones and bad ones.

Have you ever witnessed somebody moving through a rough moment in their life and you look at the choices they are making or not making, then think to yourself, this person is crazy? Perseverance can look like complete insanity to some people. Perseverance has the ability to show itself to others as stubbornness or unwillingness for that person to admit defeat. However, if you take a closer look at people that know how to persevere, there are interesting lessons to learn.

Number one, perseverance is a process. Perseverance is a process that allows certain qualities to grow like faith, strength and trust. It's a process that allows you to build deep hope for something in the future. These are powerful qualities that get built strong only through the process of perseverance. The more that you can move through this process of perseverance, the deeper your faith is built, the bigger your trust is built, the more your hope is built, and these are all phenomenal qualities to possess.

More importantly, not only are those qualities going to be built inside of you, but anytime you're moving through an obstacle or a difficulty, if you take a look around, there are probably several other people that are there to support you while you're going through perseverance. The process of perseverance creates a two for one scenario. Not only is your ability to grow through this process going to build trust, faith and hope inside of you, but more importantly, it also allows you to build faith, trust, and hope in other people that are supporting you. As a result, you will become stronger in your character when the next obstacle or the next problem comes your way. Or, you may get the benefit of helping somebody else in a similar circumstance.

The second thing that you need to become aware of as you move through this process of perseverance is that you will hit against the boundary of your capacity. In other words, you may feel like you are unable to keep moving forward. When you hit the boundary of your capacity, something negative is going to come at you. The negative things that will come at you are negative emotions like fear, anger, worry and anxiety. These are times of uncertainty. When you have fear, anger, and uncertainty coming at you, it produces the opportunity for faith, hope, and trust to get built. Most people buckle under the negative pressure. They never allow perseverance to finish its work. They never become mature, and they never produce a strong character. Trust the process. Trust that your positive emotions carry more weight than the negative ones. Trust that you will become who you are predestined to become.

∞

Empower Thought

As you move through perseverance, the truth of your real character will reveal itself. This is how real and radical growth happens. Pay attention to the negative forces that are coming at you and recognize that those negative forces produce resistance that allows deep trust, faith, and hope to grow. It's just like going in the gym and lifting weights. You need resistance, and you need heavier weights in order to grow a new muscle, and so the same thing is true for you with this word perseverance.

Questions to Ponder

1. When you think of what is going on in the world, what does this word make you think about? Describe in detail.
2. When you think about this word, how could it impact you and the relationships in your life? Describe in detail.
3. When you think about this word, what is stopping you from growing in this area of your life? Describe in detail.

Word 39: PERSPECTIVE

Definition

Aiding the vision; relating to, employing or seeing in perspective

Bible Verse

Do not let your hearts be troubled. You believe in God, believe also in me. My father's house has many homes. If that were not so, would I have told you that I am going there to prepare a place for you? And if I go and prepare a place for you, I will come back and take you with me that you may also be where I am. You know the way to the place that I am going.
~ John 14:1-4 NIV

Food for Thought

I cannot change the direction of the wind but I can adjust my sails to reach my destination. ~ Anonymous

Contemplation

The word perspective gives us an enormous opportunity to change the way that we live in the world. In order to have proper perspective, we need to ensure that we live in a way that is flexible and dynamic. Not rigid.

Has anyone ever told you to, "put things into perspective"? We've all had that said to us and we've probably said it to a lot of other people as well. The reason this is a good reminder is because in the midst of challenges and struggles, our vision can become impaired. We get shortsighted vision and can only see the problems that are starring back at us. Putting things into perspective allows us to look at the larger picture.

Putting things into perspective allows you to pull back the lens of life and see with a wider angle. It is important at moments like this to pause and reflect on some simple questions that allow the lens to get wider by looking at your past, present and future.

- Where have you come from?
- Where are you right now?
- Where are you going into the future?
- Based on your past experiences, how have things worked out for you?
- Based on your current experiences of what's going on, what is working for you?
- And based on your future hopes and dreams, what is it the next thing you need to do?

If you can have this perspective of looking into your past, looking at your present and looking into the future, it gives you this long view that allows you to put things into perspective.

- What is the direction that you're going?
- What is the trajectory that you're going relative to the overall vision of your life?

You see all of us have beliefs. All of us hold onto those beliefs. And if we're not careful, and if we don't have the ability to pull ourselves back and look at the perspective of the world and look at the perspective of our life in the world, it will be very challenging for us. You'll have what's called tunnel vision. You'll just constantly do, do, do and all of a sudden you have certain results but you don't know why.

So this word perspective is extremely important. When you look at your current circumstances right now, develop the perspective to ask your self:

- What were your past behaviors that brought you here?
- What are your current behaviors that are keeping you here?
- If you don't change something, then where will you ultimately end up?

∞

Empower Thought

That's the perspective you need to have, past, present, and future. Also, these questions will allow you to gain perspective on the amount of time it may take for you to get to where you are trying to go in life. Perspective is a point of view. It's looking at the past, the present and the future, the long view of your life.

Questions to Ponder

1. When you think of what is going on in the world, what does this word make you think about? Describe in detail.
2. When you think about this word, how could it impact you and the relationships in your life? Describe in detail.
3. When you think about this word, what is stopping you from growing in this area of your life? Describe in detail.

Word 40: POWER

Definition

Ability or right to control people or things; the ability to produce an effect

Bible Verse

Since the creation of the world, God's invisible qualities, his eternal power and divine nature have been clearly seen, being understood from what has been made so that people are without excuse. ~ Romans 1:20 NIV

Food for Thought

You have the power to change your life at any given moment. Never forget that. ~ Anonymous

Contemplation

There is truth to the idea that you have the power within you to change your life. Under the right conditions the power can come from within you to change your life and the trajectory of your life forever. I do not agree with the definition of power as the ability to have power over people. There are too many people seeking this type of positional power. There are too many people who pursue power positions and enjoy overpowering other people. Instead, I would like to challenge you to think about the word power as the ability produce an effect.

I believe that humans are living, breathing miracles designed with a very unique ability to create and produce. I believe that power is an unbelievable gift that's been given to us that needs to be respected while also nurtured. Humans have the capacity to produce, to create, to think and use our senses to grow and shape the way that we live in the world.

When contemplating the word power, lets see how it relates to human capacity. In order to gain a better understanding of how power relates to your capacity, it will be important to know what capacity is. Often, while discussing capacity, people will confuse capacity with capability. There is a big difference between your capabilities and your capacity. Capabilities are your ability to do something. Capacity is how much of it can you do. Or in other words, capacity looks at how much power you have. How much horsepower do you have right now inside of you in your body, in your mind, in your heart, and in your spirit? The power inside of you allows you to produce and to create things and that is your capacity.

I was introduced to a great book years ago that I have since read several times called "Power vs. Force" by David R. Hawkins, M.D., Ph.D. In the book he examined the hidden determinants of human behavior. He categorized these hidden determinants and noticed that there is a difference between people who use power and people who use force.

Force is you having to use your energy to force something to happen. When you force something to happen you are basically depleting all of your energy in an attempt to do something. You're going to force yourself into a sale. You're going to force yourself into a relationship. You're going to force yourself into a building. Whatever it is, you have to do exude energy that applies the force. Once the force is applied, your energy is usually depleted.

Power, on the other hand, is different than force. You don't lose your energy when you're using power. Power is when you have the energy, you have the capacity and you are able to just sit in it. You're not depleting anything. Power is like gravity. The sun has so much gravity and so much gravitational pull to it, there's so much power sitting inside the mass of the sun that the earth and all the other planets in our solar system gravitate and are pulled around the sun in a gravitational pull. The sun isn't forcing the earth to come towards it; the sun is just doing what the sun does. The sun is just being what the sun is, and when the sun is being what the sun is everything else just comes around it because of what it is. It's not exuding force or getting rid of force, it's just being what it is and everything gravitates around it.

The same thing is true for you. Real power comes from knowing who you are, your purpose, your passions, and knowing your place in this world. That's where the real power comes from. The moment you can move in that power, you increase your capacity to enhance yourself and others around you.

∞

Empower Thought

If you take the time to pause and reflect on this word power, your capacity will increase, your energy will increase, and the momentum in your life will increase as well. People will recognize you have a different energy about you. They'll recognize that you stand in a position of power without having to be forceful. You just being able to be the real you will become a gravitational pull for other people. They will want to be around you because they'll recognize that you're sitting in the power of truth to who you are and your purpose for being here. That's the truth of this word power.

Questions to Ponder

1. When you think of what is going on in the world, what does this word make you think about? Describe in detail.
2. When you think about this word, how could it impact you and the relationships in your life? Describe in detail.
3. When you think about this word, what is stopping you from growing in this area of your life? Describe in detail.

Word 41: PRAYER

Definition

A set order of words used in praying; an address or a petition to God or a god in a word or in thought

Bible Verse

Therefore, I tell you, whatever you ask for in prayer, believe that you have received it and it will be yours. ~ Mark 11:24 NIV

Food for Thought

If you only pray when you are in trouble, then you are in trouble.
~ Anonymous

Contemplation

When do you lean on prayer the most? Good times or in bad times? A lot of us tend to go to prayer when we're experiencing trouble, pain or hardships. That seems absolutely normal to do. In trying to understand the power of this word prayer, we need to recognize that we should aim for prayer to become a daily behavior, a belief system and a strong foundation for us. Prayer has absolute power to shift and change the way that you live in the world. Prayer can definitely change the way you see things in the world, the way you hear things in the world, and most definitely the way you feel things in the world.

If we go back to the dictionary definitions, it talks about an address or petition to God or a god in word or in thought. I'm not here to tell you what you should believe. I think that everyone at some moment in time recognizes that there's probably something bigger going on. All of us have had our backs up against the wall. We've all experienced problems or difficulties. In those moments of challenge, you will have a desire or need to reach out to someone or something bigger than you looking for guidance and solutions to your problems.

Prayer is the capacity to have and utilize a deep faith, solid beliefs, and hope in something pure. We all know that if we have to rely only on ourselves to get through all of the problems that we face in the world, our capacity will be extremely limited. One of the ways to increase your capacity in life is through prayer. I believe that prayer is an opportunity for you to tap into some hidden capacity that's inside you, to find some hidden beliefs that are there with the power to get you through struggles in life. Prayer will increase your perseverance, patience and clarity of purpose.

- When was the last time you prayed?
- What did you pray for?
- Do you pray in bad times?
- Do you pray in good times?
- How frequent do you pray?
- How long and deep do your prayers go?
- Do you pray for others?
- Do you pray more for spiritual growth or financial growth?

I want to challenge you in the way you pray. Prayer has more power when it is coming from a state of gratitude. Be grateful for your opportunity to be a living, breathing miracle. Be grateful for your ability to find your passion, your purpose and be grateful for the ability to pursue it. This will create a solid belief system that lays an unbreakable foundation of trust between you and God. When the storms of life come, you will not be taken away.

∞

Empower Thought

When you move into prayer, it's an opportunity to let go of all the negativity that's in your life. When you let go of the negativity it makes room for the positive. Prayer develops positive beliefs, positive faith, positive trust and positive hope in yourself, in others, and most importantly, in God. Ultimately, your purity of heart grows. Allow prayer to develop into a behavior for you every single day, of every single week, of every single month, of every single year, for the rest of your life and the way that you live in the world will begin to change. I dare you to find out!

Questions to Ponder

1. When you think of what is going on in the world, what does this word make you think about? Describe in detail.
2. When you think about this word, how could it impact you and the relationships in your life? Describe in detail.
3. When you think about this word, what is stopping you from growing in this area of your life? Describe in detail.

Word 42: PURPOSE

Definition

The reason why something is done or used; the aim or intention of something; what a person is trying to do or become

Bible Verse

For it is God who works in you to will and to act in order to fulfill his good purpose. ~ Philippians 2:13 NIV

Food for Thought

If you're alive there's a purpose for your life. ~ Rick Warren

Contemplation

All of us, at least one moment in our life, will ask the question, what is my purpose? What is my calling? What should I being doing with my life? I believe this is one of the most powerful questions you can ever ask yourself. That's why I love this quote from Rick Warren, he said, "If you're alive there's a purpose for your life".

I have always loved the idea of looking at a human and knowing that there's a DNA strand inside of every single cell of your body. That DNA strand, if you had the opportunity to pluck it out of any one of your trillions of cells and pull it apart, it would measure approximately six feet long. DNA is comprised of four characters, A, C, T, and G that ultimately make up a sequence code of three billion characters. Every single one of your DNA strands, inside of every single cell in your body, has this unique series of character codes, three billion characters in length. If you read one character per second of your DNA sequence code, it would take you 91 years to read the story of you. BOOM! Right there is proof that if you're alive, there is a reason for your life. There is a very specific purpose that you're here for. There is no greater thing to ponder or pray about than why are you here and what is your purpose for being here.

I honestly believe that you are a living, breathing miracle and that you are here for a very significant reason. You are here to make a difference and you deserve to find out what is your significance. I believe that you were created by God and for God with a unique DNA sequence code that provides the blueprint for your unique talents.

I believe that every single human has a very specific purpose and role to play. Think about it - there has never been a human before you that had your exact DNA code, and there's no human currently living that has your DNA code. This is evidence that you have something unique that's encoded in your DNA, which is packed into every single cell of your body. You have something unique that is encoded in your DNA that allows you to fulfill your purpose for living. I think every single human has a unique purpose that's designed in some way to impact and benefit all of humanity.

- Why were you born?
- What is your purpose?
- What do you believe are your unique talents encoded into your DNA?
- Do you believe that if you pursued those unique talents, they would be of benefit to others?
- How do you pursue your purpose and unique talents?

You're maybe going to be alive on earth for 60, 70, 80, 90, or a 100 years. Some people less than that, some people more than that. But maybe for 80 years you get your shot at being here on earth. Take those 80 years against the backdrop of all of humanity and that's not a random scenario. That's not some freaky set of circumstances that you're here. The fact that you can think about it, contemplate it, have a conversation about it, already starts pointing to the truth that there's a very unique purpose for you being here. Spend some serious time contemplating your purpose. Contemplate what are your unique gifts, what are your unique talents and how could you, if you paid attention to them, and if you actually built the capacity around them, how would they impact all of humanity. And also on the flip side, if you didn't pay attention to it, and if you didn't pursue it, how could that also impact all of humanity for the rest of eternity. Think about something that is eternal and then think about your role in that eternity.

∞

Empower Thought

I challenge you to look at your purpose relative of a backdrop of all of eternity. Do you have the confidence? Do you have the stamina? Do you have the strength? Do have the perseverance? Do you have the ability to stand on a foundation of truth to look at the backdrop of all of eternity, to look at your purpose for being here? I think that if you do, you'll really start to unpack the truth that is inside this word purpose. How big is your game?

Questions to Ponder

1. When you think of what is going on in the world, what does this word make you think about? Describe in detail.
2. When you think about this word, how could it impact you and the relationships in your life? Describe in detail.
3. When you think about this word, what is stopping you from growing in this area of your life? Describe in detail.

Word 43: SELF-CONTROL

Definition

Control over your feelings or actions; restraint exercised over one's impulses, emotions, or desires

Bible Verse

Put to death, therefore, whatever belongs to your earthly nature. Set away morality, impurity, lust, evil desires and greed, which is idolatry.
~ Colossians 3:5 NIV

Food for Thought

What lies in your power to do also lies in your power not to do. ~ Aristotle

Contemplation

Self-control is controlling yourself from doing something that you want to do but you know is not going to be beneficial to you. You need self-control to limit your temptations that can lead you down a path that can harm you and shrink your capacity to be effective in the world. It is the restraint and control over your feelings, over your actions and over your impulses. We all have plenty of examples to share of how we lose our self-control.

I believe self-control is a battle that is being waged in every single human on this planet since the beginning of time. It is a battle between your ego and your spirit. Your ego is predominantly driven by external desires while your spirit is driven from within. The ego can bring a lot of force with it to go after the desires of the eyes. The ego brings some very dangerous and debilitating negative emotions. What happens with your ego is that it sees something externally and it begins to desire those things, whether it's a new car, a new house, new clothes, more money, fame, or more of anything that triggers your senses. You see something, you hear something, you smell something, or you taste something. That starts to trigger the desires inside of you of these external things. Then you start to get driven towards wanting to go and have them – more and more. You have to be very careful because those external desires, when you see other people have those things, it opens up the opportunity for anger, envy and greed to creep in. It's okay to have goals, aspirations and ambitions, but where you have to be careful is not to fall over into the canyon of desires. You have to know how to pull yourself back.

Self-control is an important word to pause and reflect on. When you get in control, you become more driven by your spirit instead of your ego. The spirit is more of an internal process. Your spirit is being able to understand yourself. Your spirit wants you to pursue your true purpose for life. That usually comes with limiting the ego's desires for external things and increasing your desire to want to become better internally. It's things that you typically can't see. They're not necessarily triggered by your senses, but all of a sudden, if you can get to that point of recognizing your spirit, you're not going to lose yourself downstream in the river of your ego.

- Are you in control or are you out of control?
- How do you develop your self-control?
- Would other people describe you as having self-control?

∞

Empower Thought

If you're driven more by your ego and the desires of the world you may end up walking down the path of being out of control. You need to have faith in yourself, belief in yourself and trust in yourself through self-control. That way you won't be tempted to do the other things that can cause harm to you financially, physically, emotionally, mentally or spiritually. Self-control is a tough quality to develop. I know that we all battle with self-control. With self-control you have an opportunity to be more in control, more internally driven, have a better understanding of who you are and your purpose for being here. I would rather be in control and in tune with my spirit than be driven by my ego, which is out of control. Move yourself in, get in control, and your self-control will grow.

Questions to Ponder

1. When you think of what is going on in the world, what does this word make you think about? Describe in detail.
2. When you think about this word, how could it impact you and the relationships in your life? Describe in detail.
3. When you think about this word, what is stopping you from growing in this area of your life? Describe in detail.

Word 44: SPIRIT

Definition

The force within a person that is believed to give the body life, energy and power; the inner quality, or nature of a person

Bible Verse

But the fruit of the spirit is love, joy, peace, patience, kindness, goodness and faithfulness. ~ Galatians 5:22 NIV

Food for Thought

It is not the strength of the body that counts, but the strength of the spirit.
~ J.R.R. Tolkien

Contemplation

Spirit makes something come alive in all of us. You have the spirit of life inside of you right now – do you believe that? Do you contemplate that? Do you honor your spirit? Spirit is a force, it is energy and it has incredible power associated with it. Too often we do not honor our spirit enough or think about ways to enhance it. When we talk about spirit we also talk about the fruit of the spirit. The fruit of the spirit can be love, joy, peace, patience, kindness, goodness, gentleness, faithfulness and self-control. You can judge a tree by the fruit that it produces. Now is the time for some radical reality.

- Do you produce love daily?
- Do you produce joy daily?

- Do you produce peace daily?
- Do you produce patience daily?
- Do you produce kindness daily?
- Do you produce goodness daily?
- Do you produce faithfulness daily?
- Do you produce gentleness daily?
- Do you produce self-control daily?

You know spirit-filled people when you meet them because you can feel them. You get the sense that something is totally different when you're around them. You may feel trust or love or joy or patience. You can't help but feel good when you get around somebody that is more spirit-based than ego-based. You would recognize the difference if you're sitting in the presence of someone that was more spirit-based versus someone that was more ego-based.

If you look at the dictionary definition, spirit is the inner quality. This is hard to measure and it is hard to put a finger on it. For a lot of people it becomes hard to find the absolute truth of how to grow that inner part of you called spirit. But this word spirit is so important. It is a force. It is energy, and it is absolute power that sits within you. You can recognize it within you when have an experience that triggers your spirit. It may be something that you hear, whether it's a song, whether it's a movie, whether it's a bird, or your loved one's voice, whatever it is, your spirit comes a little bit more alive. It makes you sit up a little bit more. It makes you feel good. It makes you start to move a little bit more. It creates an instant change inside of you and the way that you live in the world begins to change. Recognize that you have a spirit that sits inside of you. Recognize also, that you have a battle between your ego and your spirit every single day.

- What would happen in your life if you gave more attention to the force and energy and power called your spirit in your life?
- What if you honored your spirit a little bit more each day? What would happen?
- Would your life be more positive or more negative?
- What if you're a little bit more grateful for your spirit daily?
- What if you recognized it and tried to grow it?
- How strong is your relationship with your spirit?

∞

Empower Thought

A wise man once said that, "God wouldn't let you have a lick of the ice cream cone if you were not meant to have the whole thing." Who wants just one little lick of an ice cream cone? One little experience in life can plant the seed for your spirit to come alive. You should be driven by a desire to grow your spirit every single minute of every single hour, of every single day, of every single week, of every single month, of every single year, for the rest of your life. It could probably be one of the greatest things you could ever do for your life today and tomorrow. The way you live in the world will begin to change immediately, the moment you begin to pay attention to and build your relationship with your spirit. You will recognize that it has enormous power, enormous energy, it is a magical force and it is a gift from God. The fact that you can see and hear, and touch, and move, and think, and contemplate, and have a conversation about all these things, ego and spirit and compassion, all these different words, lets you know that there's something that's inside of you. I think that it a mysterious and magical gift, for which I am eternally grateful for.

Questions to Ponder

1. When you think of what is going on in the world, what does this word make you think about? Describe in detail.
2. When you think about this word, how could it impact you and the relationships in your life? Describe in detail.
3. When you think about this word, what is stopping you from growing in this area of your life? Describe in detail.

Word 45: STRENGTH

Definition

The quality or state of being physically strong; the capacity for exertion or endurance

Bible Verse

I can do all things through Him who gives me strength.
~ Philippians 4:13 NIV

Food for Thought

The struggle your in today is developing the strength you need for tomorrow. ~ Anonymous

Contemplation

We all have problems. We all are struggling with something today. If we can put our current struggles and our current problems into the proper perspective as it relates to this word strength, we will recognize that what we're currently going through is actually developing us in a way that's going to provide us more strength tomorrow. The struggle is increasing your capacity to have more endurance tomorrow.

Let's look at how the word capacity relates to the word strength. For a long time I have been studying the difference between people's capabilities and their capacities. I think there's a big difference between capability and capacity. Most people when they go to learn something new focus more on increasing their capabilities. For example, most people try learning to increase their capabilities to sell, or market, or communicate, or lead, or manage, or entrepreneurship, etc. All of these things are great, but capabilities will only get you so far. Your capabilities will always hit against the boundary of your capacity. Capacity focuses on how much of a capability can you do. Strength is the capacity to endure long enough to increase your capabilities.

The same thing is true if I were to give you an example of lifting weights. If you went to the gym and started lifting dumbbells, the first question would be, "Are you capable of lifting a dumbbell with your bicep?" If the answer is yes, the very next thing that you're going to look at is, "What is your capacity? How heavy is the dumbbell? How many reps of the dumbbell can you do? For how long can you do them for?" This is capacity for strength training. The same thing is true for you and in your life with this word strength. If it's the quality or state of being able to endure, then you have to look at your capacity. Are your capabilities hitting the boundary of your capacities?

- Do you understand the difference between capability and capacity?
- Do people see you as strong?
- Do you enjoy strength training?
- Do you strength train your body?
- Do you strength train your mind?
- Do you strength train your emotions?
- Do you strength train your thoughts?
- Do you strength train your spirit?

∞

Empower Thought

Focus on building your capacity for strength. If you do, you will become more effective and you'll become more efficient. You will be able to do more things in life with less energy. Strength provides a solid foundation and you will become more reliable for people, you'll provide comfort and protection for people, you'll be seen as a place of refuge. You will be able to persevere life's struggles as you build this word strength. Sit and ponder strength and try to unpack the truth of it. It will lead you to question your capacity, how much of these things can you do, how much of these capabilities are inside of you, how effective are you, how efficient are you, and for how long can you do it? I think that if you understand the difference between capability and capacity, you'll see that your strength will begin to increase and the way that you live in the world will definitely change.

Questions to Ponder

1. When you think of what is going on in the world, what does this word make you think about? Describe in detail.
2. When you think about this word, how could it impact you and the relationships in your life? Describe in detail.
3. When you think about this word, what is stopping you from growing in this area of your life? Describe in detail.

Word 46: SUCCESS

Definition

The fact of getting or achieving wealth, respect or fame; correct or desired result of an attempt

Bible Verse

If the axe is dull, and it's edge unsharpened, more strength is needed, but skill will bring success. ~ Ecclesiastes 10:10 NIV

Food for Thought

Success is not final, failure is not fatal, it is the courage to continue that counts. ~ Winston Churchill

Contemplation

Success is not a destination. You don't just arrive at success and magically it's all over. Success is a journey. Success is a process of becoming somebody. It is also worth pointing out the flip side of success that says failure is not fatal. Most of us, when we fail or if we are currently failing in our life, view it as a fatal position. We may even label ourselves as being unsuccessful. We need to be careful how we, number one, define this word success and number two, how we measure this word success.

Go back to the definition of success and it says the fact of getting, or achieving wealth, respect, and fame. Careful, there is some danger that is built into the average definition of success. There is danger in the way that most people would define success. If you had the chance to go around the world and ask different people in different countries, "What would you consider success?" and "Who would you consider to have led a successful life?" You would have all kinds of names that start to rise to the top. They are usually people that are rich and famous by the worlds standard. Yet there are 7+ billion humans on earth and at some moment in time, we are all a total success. It depends on perspective and the story we tell ourselves about success.

People that are rich or famous follows along with the dictionary definition that you've achieved some level of wealth, or fame. And unfortunately, that's how most people would define it, and that's how most people would measure it. Therefore, if you haven't attained financial mastery, and if you're not rich and famous, then somehow your life is not successful. I just don't think that there's truth in that definition or that way of measuring.

Instead, I want to challenge you to look at the result of an attempt. Success is not final and failure is not fatal. Your life is a constant up and down. The fact that you are alive is evidence of success. The fact that you were born a living, breathing miracle, has so much success written into it, that you don't get yourself enough credit for who you are and your purpose for being here.

There are many areas of your life I would suggest have been and continue to be areas of success. It could be that success is being able to build and grow certain relationships, or your family, or your ability to acquire knowledge, or your ability to understand your spirit or your purpose. If you have had many great ups and downs in your life, then you are a success to me. You have the power to educate others from your life experiences. It is all in the way you view the word success. Success is your ability to move through life, your ability to learn from it, your ability to grow from it, your ability to communicate to somebody else what you've learned from it. You have something to offer, to so many people, that you are so successful beyond measure. It's just the way that you measure it, or the way that you define it, that you would consider yourself not a success.

- How do you define success?
- Who do you view as having a successful life?
- What areas of your life is a success?
- Do you want more success in life? Why?
- What does success bring?
- Do you recognize little things as successful?

∞

Empower Thought

You see, I think there's so much to this word success. Every single day you are moving through a process of becoming more. The fact that you continue to move through life is a success. Take the time to pause and reflect on the word success, how you define it and how you measure it. I believe that you will become more successful on how you see things in the world, how you hear things in the world, and how you live in the world.

Questions to Ponder

1. When you think of what is going on in the world, what does this word make you think about? Describe in detail.
2. When you think about this word, how could it impact you and the relationships in your life? Describe in detail.
3. When you think about this word, what is stopping you from growing in this area of your life? Describe in detail.

Word 47: TIME

Definition

The thing that is measured as seconds, minutes, hours, days, years, etc.

Bible Verse

There is a time for everything and a season for every activity under the heavens. A time to be born and a time to die. A time to plant and a time to uproot. A time to kill and a time to heal. A time to tear down and a time to build. A time to weep and a time to laugh. A time to mourn and a time to dance. A time to scatter stones and a time to gather them up. A time to embrace and a time to refrain from embracing. A time to search and a time to give up. A time to keep and a time to throw away. A time to tear and a time to mend. A time to be silent and a time to speak. A time to love and a time to hate. A time for war and a time for peace. ~ Ecclesiastes 3:1-8 NIV

Food for Thought

All great achievements require time. ~ Maya Angelo

Contemplation

All of our life experiences occur over time. That's why this word time becomes extremely important to understand so that you can get a full lesson of truth that lies inside of time. If you get your perspective right on time, then all of a sudden the way that you live in the world will begin to change and your purpose for living over time will begin to change as well.

If we go back to the definitions they use the word "measured" for time. Time is a measured period or a measurable period. This is an important place to pause because a lot of people confuse what time actually is. Time is nothing more than a measurement. It can be a measurement in seconds, minutes, hours, days, years, etc. If I were to say the number "168" to you, what would that number represent? "168". Well, it can represent a lot of different things, but as it relates to time, it's a measurement of time. In this case, "168" only represents a measurement of the number of hours in a week. There are 168 hours in a week. I could also say that there are seven days in a week. However, "168" only represents the number of hours and therefore it's just a measurement of time. The important question becomes, what do you do with that time?

A lot of people confuse the meaning of time and they'll associate it to something that it is not. For example, I've asked this question all over the world, I will ask, "What is time?" Most people say, "Time is money." That is a nice cliché that sounds great, however, time is not money. If you say that time is money and build that into your belief system, then it starts to distort the real meaning of the word time. It also begins to devalue your understanding of what the word time means, if you only associate it with money. It is a very low capacity way to look at the real value that's hidden inside of this word time.

If you limit time to money, then part of you're belief system will be driven by money. You will lose sight of all the other great benefits that come with time. For example, let's choose another way of looking at time. Since time is going to move anyways and you're not in control of that, who are you becoming over time? Most people get discouraged looking at time as a road to travel down towards their hopes, dreams and goals. For most, it seems to take too much time to arrive at a desired destination. This is why time is a great backdrop to the story of who you are becoming over time. The only way to evolve and progress is --- over time!

- Time allows you to evolve
- Time allows you to progress
- Time allows you to slow down
- Time allows you to learn
- Time allows you to build trust with others
- Time allows you to lead
- Time allows you to influence
- Time allows you to empower others

Time actually gives you an opportunity to slow down. If you had the ability to slow down you may find that your ability to accomplish things could speed up. If you learn this hidden secret to time, a lot more things could get done with a lot less effort and during a lot less time. Most people feel like they're running out of time, if you were able to just pause, you may realize that you have an abundance of time. You can reprioritize the way that you view time.

∞

Empower Thought

If you looked at time as an opportunity for you to grow in a relationship with you and with someone or someone else bigger than you, all of a sudden time serves a different purpose. When you have down time, you could use that time now a catalyst for you to grow. It could become a catalyst for you to grow in a relationship with somebody else or it's a catalyst for you to grow in a relationship of gratitude, to grow personally, to reflect on your life experiences. Time becomes a great learning environment, it becomes a great classroom and time becomes a great relationship builder. I want to challenge you and the way that you look at time. I challenge you to slow down in order to speed up.

Questions to Ponder

1. When you think of what is going on in the world, what does this word make you think about? Describe in detail.
2. When you think about this word, how could it impact you and the relationships in your life? Describe in detail.
3. When you think about this word, what is stopping you from growing in this area of your life? Describe in detail.

Word 48: TRANSFORMATION

Definition

Complete or major change in someone's or something's appearance; an act, or process, or an instance of transforming or being transformed

Bible Verse

Who, by the power that enables him to bring everything under his control, will transform our lowly bodies so that they will be like His glorious body.
~ Philippians 3:21 NIV

Food for Thought

Real transformation requires real honesty. If you want to move forward, you need to get real with yourself. ~ Bryant McGill

Contemplation

Real transformation requires real honesty. Real transformation is a complete and major change. If you want to transform and have a complete or major change in your life, it's going to require you to pause, reflect and have a real conversation with yourself and about yourself. It needs to be an honest conversation about where you've come from, where you are, and ultimately, where you are trying to get to. The radical reality of transformation is that it is not a small task. It's not something that's simple and ordinary. Transformation, the definition says, is a complete and major change. It's bigger than just a simple change. It's a major change. It's a complete change. Often times, it's unrecognizable what you've changed into. It's a complete transformation.

I would challenge yourself to think about what is the greatest transformation you could ever have in your life. For me, the greatest transformation that could ever occur for me in my life is a spiritual transformation. Transforming spiritually the way that I live in the world. A real transforming of my mind, transforming of my heart, and transforming of my spirit into something else. I am committed to become transformed and renewed in my mind, heart and in my spirit. What could be the greatest transformation that could ever occur in your life?

If you're going to get real transformation, you have to recognize that sometimes, it is a process that forces you to slow down. Also, transformation will require that you will likely need to be able to rely on others for support. You're going to have to rely on someone or something greater than yourself to move you through this entire transformation process because it takes tremendous power, courage, determination, perseverance and strength.

There are 3 physical laws of nature that will be working with you or against you on your journey.

1. The Second Law of Thermodynamics
2. The Law of Perturbation
3. The Laws of Germination & Gestation

The second law of thermodynamics says that if there is a tree that falls in the forest, the tree will begin to transform into dirt and soil over a long period of time. The law of thermodynamics says that in order for something to transform, it first has to go into decay and disorder before it reorders itself into something else. During the process of transformation, you have to recognize that something will be dying. However, this dying process creates the opportunity for something else to grow. It may be the dying off of old thoughts, beliefs, and emotions. As they die off, it makes room for new thoughts, beliefs and emotions to come to life.

The law of perturbation is like the process of a piece of coal turning into a diamond. The pressure forced onto the piece of coal allows for the disordering of the atoms of the piece of coal. Then they get reordered into a new sequence, what is now called a diamond. A piece of coal looks different than a diamond. The coal is black and you can't see through it. You could chip it away. Once it's transformed into a diamond, it's solid, it's clear, and it has tremendous strength to it. Also the value of a diamond is greater than the value of a piece of coal.

The law of germination and gestation can be seen with the example of a caterpillar turning into a butterfly. There's nothing in the body of a caterpillar that says that it could be a butterfly. Its body is cylinder. It has many legs. It crawls on the ground. It eats leaves. Once it goes into a cocoon, it too goes through the process of decay. From one thing, it reorders itself into something else, and it becomes this beautiful butterfly. One walks with legs while the other one flies with wings. They both will have a totally different vision, perspective and experience of life and the world they live in.

∞

Empower Thought

The body of a butterfly looks totally different than the body of a caterpillar. What a diamond looks like is different than what a piece of coal looks like. A tree looks different than dirt. Yet, in that process of transformation, it's one thing transforming itself into something else. I challenge you to think about what would be the greatest form of transformation you could have in your life. For me, it's a spiritual transformation because you can look at each of those processes, what's true of each of those processes that I shared with you; coal turning to a diamond and a caterpillar turning into a butterfly, the process is irreversible. The process is irreversible. You're not going to take a diamond and turn it into a piece of coal. You're not going to take a butterfly and turn it back into a caterpillar. That's why, for me, a spiritual transformation is the greatest. If I can transform my spirit, the renewal of my mind, that would be a process that would be worthy to not have it change back to something old and less valuable. This is a moment for you to be real with yourself. That's why I love the idea that real transformation requires real honesty. If you want to move forward, you have to get real with yourself.

Questions to Ponder

143

1. When you think of what is going on in the world, what does this word make you think about? Describe in detail.
2. When you think about this word, how could it impact you and the relationships in your life? Describe in detail.
3. When you think about this word, what is stopping you from growing in this area of your life? Describe in detail.

Word 49: TRUST

Definition

Belief that someone or something is reliable, good, honest and effective; assured reliance on the character, ability, strength or truth of something or someone

Bible Verse

Trust in the Lord with all your heart and lean not on your own understanding; in all your ways submit to him and he will make your paths straight. ~ Proverbs 3:5-6 NIV

Food for Thought

The best way to find out if you can trust somebody is to just trust them. ~ Ernest Hemmingway

Contemplation

Trust is the belief or an assured reliance. This belief is an important word but so are the other parts of the definition for trust. Those are the parts that deal with trust in other people. It is difficult for most people to trust themselves, let alone to put their full trust in someone or something else.

What is your current ability to trust in someone or something outside of yourself? This question is where real opportunity for growth will occur for you. Sometimes it is other people that will give you the power and courage necessary for you to trust you. However, trust is often a shaky element that sits in the fabric of most human interactions. Most people have had trust broken. There are so many clichés around the word trust:

- Trust is earned
- Trust is given
- Trust yourself
- Trust others
- Trust can be broken
- Trust your actions
- Never trust yourself
- Never trust somebody else

There has been so much advice, sayings and misuse around the word trust that I think it can become a very difficult word to truly understand and unpack. Therefore, understanding trust begins with understanding your thoughts, beliefs, and emotions.

- Do you trust you?
- Do you trust your thoughts? Your beliefs? Your emotions?
- What evidence do you have that trusting you yields the best results for your life?
- Do you trust others?
- Who do you currently trust the most in life?

Most people cannot trust themselves and most people, if they're being completely honest with themselves, really haven't yielded good results from themselves. We've all heard people say, "Hey, trust your gut. Trust your instincts." Often times, that is just bad advice and often times, if that's all that you trust is your guts or your instincts, more than half of the time, your guts or instincts may be way off. People will also say, "Trust your heart. Just follow your heart," and sometimes that can be faulty advice as well, so you have to become aware.

Trust is built on a foundation. Trust has a foundation and it has walls that will ultimately support you as you move through life. Where do you find the greatest source of trust? What is the biggest rock that you can lean on that is so trustworthy that it is guaranteed to be there and to be a support for you every single day of every single week for the rest of your life? I think that ultimately comes from God, your creator.

- Do you trust that you were born for a purpose?
- Do you trust that God has great plans for your life? If not, why?

∞

Empower Thought

That's where trust begins for me, trusting that God created me with unique skills and talents for His purpose. Imagine being able to trust the creator of the universe with your life! WOW! If you can begin to trust in something that sits outside of you yet lives inside of you, that is a foundation you can lean against as you move through trusting yourself and others. I know it's a big challenge, but I do want you to realize that I believe and trust that you were born for a very particular purpose.

Questions to Ponder

1. When you think of what is going on in the world, what does this word make you think about? Describe in detail.
2. When you think about this word, how could it impact you and the relationships in your life? Describe in detail.
3. When you think about this word, what is stopping you from growing in this area of your life? Describe in detail.

Word 50: TRUTH

Definition

The real facts about something, the things that are true; the quality or state of being true

Bible Verse

Then you will know the truth and the truth will set you free. ~ John 8:32 NIV

Food for Thought

Three things cannot be hidden: the sun, the moon and the truth. ~ Buddha

Contemplation

What is truth and where do you find it? This is a challenge for all of us. There is so much noise in the world. Everybody has an opinion or is a self-proclaimed expert about something. With 7+ billion people on earth, cutting through all the non-sense of the world can be tough. Therefore, where you look for truth becomes just as important as how to recognize it once you hear it or see it. In my experience, people have a very hard time accepting truth. They don't know what to do with truth once they receive it. Very often, they will miss truth even when it is standing right in front of them.

- How do you know if something is true or false?
- What test do you use to determine if something is true or false?
- Who is the most truthful person you know?
- What is the most powerful truth you have heard in your life?

Also, some people will ask for true feedback about their lives, yet discard the feedback, even if it is true. They'll say, "Hey, give me some feedback," or "Give me some observations about my life." And the moment you start providing that truthful feedback, they start to make rationalizations and justifications for their behaviors. It is an immediate denial and lack of accountability for their life. So while most people are trying to seek truth, a lot of times when they start to receive it, they don't know how to handle it.

- Have you ever asked for true feedback?
- How do you handle true feedback – the good and the bad?
- Do you feel comfortable providing true feedback to others? Why or Why not?

Finding truth is absolutely important. Your life will change the moment you accept the truth about why you were born and for what purpose.

- What is true for you?
- Why do you believe you were born?
- What do you believe your purpose is?
- Why are you here?
- Why is your DNA so unique to you?
- What are the true passions for your life?
- What truth does your ego tell you about you?
- What truth does your sprit tell you about you?

∞

Empower Thought

So what is the absolute truth for you? Truth can also open up other words to observe like clarity and purity. You know when you have stumbled on the truth when it provides you with a clarity and that clarity makes you feel more pure. Things that are false typically make you feel dirty, tired, unfocused and un-motivated. There is so much opportunity to find the pure, clean, clear truth for you and your life. I hope that you take the time to find it.

Questions to Ponder

1. When you think of what is going on in the world, what does this word make you think about? Describe in detail.
2. When you think about this word, how could it impact you and the relationships in your life? Describe in detail.
3. When you think about this word, what is stopping you from growing in this area of your life? Describe in detail.

Word 51: WISDOM

Definition

Knowledge that is gained by having many life experiences; a wise attitude, belief or course of action

Bible Verse

For where you have envy and selfish ambition, there you will find disorder in every evil practice. But the wisdom that comes from heaven is first of all pure, then peace loving, considerate, submissive, full of mercy and good fruit, impartial and sincere. Peacemakers who sow in peace reap a harvest of righteousness. ~ James 3:16-18 NIV

Food for Thought

Do not let your happiness depend on something that you may lose. ~ CS Lewis

Contemplation

Wisdom is knowledge that is gained by having many experiences in life. That statement about wisdom carries a couple of key phrases, "many experiences" and "in life". Since we all have had many experiences in life, does that make us all wise? The answer is yes and no. The real challenge with wisdom comes in the process of pausing, reflecting and learning from those many experiences in life and pulling out the lessons, the knowledge, the patterns and our belief systems. That is the hard work of gaining wisdom that most are unwilling to do. Life gives us many experiences and life is a great teacher if we pause to look at where the wisdom can be pulled out of. Wisdom can most often get pulled out of our self-awareness of our belief systems that serve us or destroy us.

The second part of the definition says that wisdom having a wise attitude, belief or course of action. I think that those last three words "course of action" are important. Are you pro-actively seeking wisdom? You can't just be in the process of only reading books, listening to podcasts or watching videos to gain wisdom. You actually have to go through a process of taking what you learn and then applying it to your life. You need to actively apply the information in order to unlock the wisdom. Taking what you learn and applying it immediately in your life is where the real experiences come from. That's where the hidden part of wisdom lies. Wisdom is found in your experiences. You learn something, you apply it and then you learn from that experience. And then you evaluate, adjust and gain clarity. Then you apply the new lessons that you learned and you continue moving forward. That's a course of action for wisdom.

People have different intentions for acquiring knowledge or seeking wisdom. Knowledge and wisdom are very different words with different processes. A lot of people want to acquire knowledge purely for their own self-interest. They're doing it for a competitive advantage. They're doing it merely to make more money for themselves or their business. They're doing it to get ahead. They're doing it only for self-improvement. This process is shortsighted and is a very limiting process of gaining wisdom.

Wisdom on the other hand, is moving from a process of not thinking of yourself as the sole reason for acquiring wisdom, to wanting to empower other people with your wisdom. There is a big difference in the intention. The intention for one is to acquire knowledge for an unfair competitive advantage so that you can make more money. The other is to acquire wisdom so that you can progress though life in a way that you become of service to other people. The latter is a much higher law, much higher principle, and much bigger capacity-building truth of wisdom. A question that you need to ask yourself is what guides you more:

- Your desire to acquire knowledge so that you can appear smart and gain that competitive advantage ... or
- Your desire to acquire wisdom so that you can impact other people's lives?

∞

Empower Thought

Knowledge is often driven by economic profit and wisdom is often driven by human profit. Wisdom is driven by human profit and the need to want to benefit other people. I challenge you to take a look at your life experiences. I challenge you to take a look at what lane do you drive down most often - the knowledge lane or the wisdom lane? Wisdom is a higher principle. It's a higher law and I guarantee that if you move down this lane of wisdom, your capacity would begin to grow. Your influence would begin to grow. And the way that you live in the world would definitely begin to change.

Questions to Ponder

1. When you think of what is going on in the world, what does this word make you think about? Describe in detail.
2. When you think about this word, how could it impact you and the relationships in your life? Describe in detail.
3. When you think about this word, what is stopping you from growing in this area of your life? Describe in detail.

Word 52: WORK

Definition

A job or activity that you do regularly, especially to earn money; activity in which one exerts strength or faculties to do or perform something

Bible Verse

Whatever you do, work at it with all of your heart, as working for the Lord, not for human masters. ~ Colossians 3:23 NIV

Food for Thought

Work to live. Do not live to work. ~ Anonymous

Contemplation

Work to live. Do not live to work. These statements capture an important distinction between work and a job. Too often, people associate the word work with a job. People will often say, "I have to go to work this week," or "I have to go to my job." I want to challenge you to not think of work as a job. I don't want you to associate it to the word job because the word job carries with it too many negative emotions. Soon, you begin to attach the negative emotions about a "job" to your "work".

This is a major challenge for most people. Wherever I go in the world, people always seem to have anxiety and fear associated with their job that they call work. They always want to know how to get out of their job and go do something that they really enjoy doing. In other words, they would rather quit their job to pursue their life's work, or their calling in life.

- What is your life's work?
- What do you really feel called to do?
- Is your current "job" the same or different than your "life's work"?

The pattern for most people is to go to school, study a major, graduate and then get in a job in that major, hopefully. (Not the reality for most!) This job pays them money and that money begins to create a certain lifestyle for themselves. The problem is most people get trapped in their jobs because they don't want to lose the lifestyle it provides. Unfortunately, the jobs that most people take are totally out of alignment with their true calling in life or their life's work. Most will become afraid to pursue their true life's work because they believe that their lifestyle is going to go down if they pursued their life work. They create a belief system that jobs pay money and their life's work will not. That's just not the reality, but that's the story that so many people tell themselves. So they end up living quite lives of desperation, spending endless hours in a dead end job.

Your life's work has the power to change the way you live in the world. Work to live - work is not a job. However, for most, they start a job in their 20s or 30s that they end up working in for a period of years. In many cases until their 50s or 60s. They worked so hard and they tried to advance within their job function because they wanted to be able to make and save enough money so that they could retire. In other words, they were trying to break away from their job. So many people go to work in a job for their entire adult lives only to retire away from that job. Why? So they can go do what they really want to do. This cycle of jobs just makes absolutely no sense to me. Why would you pour your life into doing something for 10, 20, 30 or 40 years only to want to retire away from it? That tells me that your job is not aligned with your true life's work. Therefore, look at this word work and disassociate it with the word job from your belief system.

∞

Empower Thought

What is a life's work that you would love to be involved in? What type of life work should you be pursuing right now? A life's work so compelling that if you poured yourself into it for the rest of your life, you would never want to walk away from it or retire from it. You could say with true authenticity, this is what I'm called to do! This is my work. This is my life's work. This is my impact to humanity. This is my impact to this body of people called humanity, and I'm willing to focus all of my attention and resources towards it.

- What do you enjoy doing that would be your life's work?
- What do you enjoy learning about?
- What do you enjoy reading about?
- What do you enjoy talking to people about?
- What do you enjoy seeing yourself doing, that you would never want to retire from it?

That's your life's work – Work to Live.

Questions to Ponder

1. When you think of what is going on in the world, what does this word make you think about? Describe in detail.
2. When you think about this word, how could it impact you and the relationships in your life? Describe in detail.
3. When you think about this word, what is stopping you from growing in this area of your life? Describe in detail.

CONCLUSION

I honestly believe that you are a living breathing miracle, predestined for greatness, created by God and for God. Hopefully you recognized a pattern as you progressed through the book. Words have power. Words can build up or words can tear down. Congratulations, your capacity to change the way you live in the world has begun to increase as a result of you taking the time to pause and reflect on each of these 52 Words. It is now time to apply that learning and teach others to do the same.

Ride the Wave of Life & PlayBig!!

Jason Tyne

ABOUT THE AUTHOR

Jason Tyne is a highly experienced global educator and thought leaders trusted by the worlds #1 personal development event organizers. Jason has worked alongside some of the worlds leading experts in personal development, business, sports and entertainment including Tony Robbins, Tom Brady, Pitbull, Les Brown, Brian Tracy, Robert Kiyosaki, Nick Vujicic, Chris Gardner, Jay Abraham, Robert Herjavec and Gary Vaynerchuk. Jason has educated in several countries including the USA, Canada, Mexico, Columbia, Spain, England, Slovakia, Switzerland, Egypt, UAE, India, South Africa, Malaysia, Singapore, Vietnam, Hong Kong, Taiwan, & Australia.

Jason has a passion for radically real growth based on a solid trust and faith in God and Jesus Christ.

Made in the USA
Columbia, SC
18 July 2017